If our psalmists lived today, how would they re-pray their prayers? How would the weight of our contemporary world make them rephrase their sighs towards heaven? Yohanna Katanacho has taken upon himself to transport the ancient psalmists to the dusty and bleeding squares of the Middle East and lend them his eyes, his heart and his pen. He draws the thread that connects their mouth to the mouths of today's persevering church, but without substituting the ancient voice. This is not just one more translation of the ancient psalter – the new prayers come alongside the ancient ones as the alto joins the soprano to sing the same song in harmony.

Myrto Theocharous, PhD
Professor of Hebrew and Old Testament, Greek Bible College, Athens, Greece

Praying Through the Psalms is an extraordinary book written by a man who lives what he has written. I have known Dr Katanacho for the last twenty-six years. Our friendship began when he led me to the Lord of lords, Jesus, and since then his mentorship, friendship and spiritual example has made a huge difference in my character and ministry. This is reflected by the depth of the words written in his amazing book, and it reflects the heart and mind of the author as he encounters God through God's Word. For the readers, it is going to be a journey that they have never experienced, as it will contextualize God's Word written through the Psalms into their very own context in whatever circumstance they might be in – hard, rough, in war or persecution, or even betrayed!

Through 150 prayers, Dr Katanacho brings the Psalms home to each and every one of us. Since I had the privilege of reading them both in Arabic and now in English, the words written by the psalmist have reminded me many times to think before I judge people and before I blame God for circumstances I go through in life. The new depth that this book has given to the Psalms has given me a stronger belief in God as a friend who understands me well in my everyday situations as he accompanies me in them all the time. Special thanks to Dr Katanacho, my friend and old-time neighbour, and colleague at the Alliance Church and at the Bethlehem Bible College, where I am honoured to serve alongside him in different capacities.

Rev Jack Y. Sara, PhD
President, Bethlehem Bible College

It's been said that the Psalms were the place where Christians used to learn how to pray and how to praise God. Whether or not it was ever true, it isn't generally true now. But it is where Yohanna Katanacho has been learning to pray and to praise over a number of years. It has led him to compose his own praises and prayers modeled on the psalms, one by one. There are at least three ways we can employ Katanacho's prayers and praises to God's glory and to our own blessing: we can simply use these prayers and praises as our own; we can use them as a way of identifying with our brothers and sisters in the Middle East and praying with them; and we can take these prayers and praises as models for our own prayers and praises that build from the biblical Psalms to say what we need to say to God.

John Goldingay, PhD
Professor of Old Testament, Fuller Theological Seminary, Pasadena, California, USA

Praying Through the Psalms is an important new work. The book sets forth a fresh and innovative approach to reading the Psalms by praying through the text in comprehensive and contemporary terms that are intelligible for the reader. Here we can find engagement with the Psalms and the Bible as whole, on one hand, and current challenges of life on the other.

This contextual reading of the Psalms puts a new challenge in front of us; that is, how to offer the Bible in people's own language. Perhaps this is the core of the Protestant reformation, that through translation normal Christians can connect with the sacred text. These contextual prayers deserve appreciation; specially as the writer is a scholar in a Palestinian context who seeks theology of his context including the challenges of the present moment.

Rev Andrea Zaki, PhD
President of the Protestant Churches of Egypt

Praying Through the Psalms

Yohanna Katanacho

© 2018 Yohanna Katanacho

Published 2018 by Langham Global Library
An imprint of Langham Creative Projects

Langham Partnership
PO Box 296, Carlisle, Cumbria CA3 9WZ, UK
www.langham.org

ISBNs:
978-1-78368-429-8 Hardback
978-1-90771-339-2 Paperback
978-1-90771-340-8 ePub
978-1-90771-390-3 Mobi
978-1-90771-391-0 PDF

British Library Cataloguing in Publication Data
A catalogue record for this book is available from the British Library

ISBN: 978-1-90771-339-2

Cover & Book Design: projectluz.com

Dedication

To Roger and Ellen Elbel,
and Dennis and Trevecca Okholm

These two families continue to model godliness and a life rooted
in prayer. I am truly blessed that God put them in my life.

Introduction

A few years ago I was going through a time of doubt and a season of despair. I felt that God was distant, and I was burnt out. I did not want to go to church or to continue serving God as an ordained minister. I felt spiritually dead.

I shared my heart with my wife. She wisely insisted that we attend a prayer conference held in Bethlehem. In the hometown of King David, I encountered the living God in a powerful way. I was convinced that I needed to spend time with the Lord. I thus decided to wake up very early every day in order to spend time alone with God.

Ever since doing my PhD dissertation on Psalms, I have had a deep respect for this text. For this reason, I decided that if I cannot meet God while studying the book of Psalms, I will not be able to find him in any other place. So I started studying the book, hoping to meet God.

As I started reading, I was challenged and inspired. I then decided to write out my prayers and post them on Facebook in order to encourage other people to pray. I was surprised by the positive response of so many people. My prayers became what I now call Facebook theology.

These prayers were originally written in poetic Arabic addressing Middle Eastern contexts. I wrote a prayer for each psalm, trying to reread it in light of the harsh realities of the contemporary Middle East. In 2015 the Arabic text was published by the Arab Israeli Bible Society.

While I was writing these psalms in Arabic, several things happened that convinced me to translate the poetic Arabic text into English. First, my friend Lucy Berry, a poet, sent me an email in the midst of violent events in Israel/Palestine. I did not know how to respond. I ended up writing the poem below to express how I felt.

> This is a season of weeping and mourning, but it is not void of hope.
> Our tears are the bridge between brutality and humanity.
> Our tears are the salty gates for seeing a different reality.
> Our tears are facing soulless nations and a parched mentality.
> Our tears are the dam preventing rivers of animosity.
> For the sake of the mourning men, cry with us to reflect your amity.

For the sake of the poor children, cry with us demanding sanity.
For the sake of lamenting mothers, refuse violence and stupidity.
Love your enemies and cry with them is the advice of divinity.
Blessing those who curse is the path to genuine spirituality.
Pouring tears of mercy and compassion is true piety.
Pray with tears, for the sake of spreading equity.
Followers of Jesus: crying is now our responsibility.
But don't cry for your friends only, cry also for your enemy.

Lucy helped me to publish the poem. Several people were encouraged by its message. In short, this incident convinced me that it is possible to put my poetic thoughts in English even though it is not my mother tongue.

Second, in 2015 I attended an international conference at which I was asked to pray. I translated one of the prayers from my Arabic book and read it at the conference. The response was beyond my expectations. Dozens of people wanted to receive a copy of that prayer, which is now found in the prayer of Psalm 120. In short, at this conference, Pieter Kwant asked me to translate a couple of prayers so that he could evaluate them. He then encouraged me to translate the whole work and publish it in English.

Third, in 2016, I became convinced that I needed to translate these prayers. However, I needed some free time in order to accomplish this task. Strangely, Christ Presbyterian Church in Edina, Minnesota, invited my family to spend a couple of months with their church. I saw God's hand in their invitation. Their generous invitation and willingness to provide a quiet place in a gorgeous environment made it possible for me to translate these prayers.

In addition, I was truly blessed by a team of friends who read my rough translations and provided helpful insights as well as indispensable linguistic comments. I especially give thanks to Marcia Mattson, Lucy Berry, Phil Sumpter, Beverley Timgren, Isobel Stevenson, and Scot Dressler. They read my manuscript and provided very helpful comments. Furthermore, I acknowledge the influence of Charles Spurgeon's sermons on my prayers.

Last, I sincerely hope that this book will encourage you to pray. When you pray, remember the church in the Middle East in your prayers.

Prayer from Psalm 1

O Lord, I dream of a perfect world like the one in Psalm 1. Its paradisiacal trees don't wither and they constantly bring forth fruit (v. 3). I dream of a day when the righteous prosper and evildoers are defeated (v. 6), when righteous people succeed but oppressors fail. The world of Psalm 1 is without conspiracies, obstacles, wars, demons, insults, and abuses. It is a world that adores love and holiness. It is empty of any defilement or malice. In this world, all people are friends and all love each other; everyone is like a green tree full of fruit that fills many baskets. In this world people don't compete but always love. It is a world of love, righteousness, equity, and vindication. It is the paradise of God for his church and the dream of every righteous person.

My dream does not come of wishful thinking but of faith. I don't wait passively for the dream or slothfully give in to evil, but I vigorously spread love and peace. I dream of a day when I myself embody this dream and become the very dream that inspires the people around me to believe and to dream.

O Lord, make your church the dream of our society and the embodiment of the kingdom of God on earth. May I be a spark that fans the flames of this vision, and may I be a bed for this wonderful dream! Open our eyes to understand that these celestial dreams will become the realities of our mornings and evenings when we are a branch in the tree of life in Christ.

~ Prayer from Psalm 2 ~

O rulers be prudent, O judges be disciplined (v. 10). Lord, many enemies desire to terminate the people of God in the Middle East. They throw bombs at churches and blast our holy sites. Their leaders are like Cain, Ahab, and Herod because they unhesitatingly seek to kill their brothers and sisters. Such policies result in widows, orphans, disabled people, and a community imprisoned by wounds and pain. Rulers and judges not only oppose celestial dreams and heavenly paths but also embrace the paths of hell. Exploitation and murder are their Bible. Their hearts are like the hearts of demons, and their bodies are infected with sin from head to toe. Where is the light of Christ? Mercy has become extinct, and there is no compassion in their hearts. They destroy unity and make smiling illegal. All the refugees and the weak ones are crying out. O Lord, your helpless boys and abandoned girls are suffering. They have been slaughtered like sheep. Didn't you promise to build your church? Why don't you listen? Palestine, Syria, Egypt and the Arab world are crying out to you. Please take away this cup. Speak to the kings and make them reconsider. Convince them to fear your anger and to stop exterminating your people.

O Lord, give us great leaders. Where is the wise Solomon? Where is David, the man after your own heart? Where are Cyrus and Daniel who spread justice and peace? O Lord, declare your holy anger against evil systems that champion murder and defilement. Have mercy on sinners but eradicate evil systems. Deliver sinners but destroy oppressive systems. Please annihilate slavery, bigotry, colonialism, neo-colonialism, chauvinism, Nazism, and dictatorships! Please, destroy every system that is rooted in sin. Why don't you reveal your divine authority and destroy wickedness in every evil system? May your people everywhere be able to live lives of quietness and tranquillity! You are the best judge!

Prayer from Psalm 3

O Lord, I want to talk frankly with you and to lay out my worries before you. There are so many who oppress me (v. 1)! My days are not happy. They are full of wounds and embarrassments. Even my son Absalom opposes me, and all those I love are blaming me. Many are raving around me.

Where can I hide? Where can I find a merciful embrace? Would you send an ambulance from heaven on this crazy day? They have killed my joy and emptied my heart of your love. O Compassionate One! Will you heal my wounds and hear my cry? Will you fill me with love and with a passion for mercy?

I will lie down and sleep in the hands of my merciful God (v. 5). I will plead for courage and determination as well as faith as I surrender into your hands. O Lord, arise (v. 7)! I sleep but you never slumber. I stop doing what is right, but you never give up or get bored. You are the source of my trust; therefore I shall not fear. You are my shield; therefore my life shall never be emptied of the joys of praise. The Lord is my saviour and my blessing whether I am awake or asleep. While I drink the cup of heartbreak and anguish, you remain my father and mother. Therefore I will sleep on your chest this day despite the betrayal of Absalom, even if my beloved son has becomes my deadly poison. I know that you are the creator of the universe. You can release me from the prison of grief, heal my wounds, drive away my terror, transform the poison within me into a healing balm, and put a cast on my broken parts. With you all things will turn out to be a blessing to your people.

∽ Prayer from Psalm 4 ∽

Know that the Lord has set apart his faithful servant (v. 3).

O Lord, athletes are distinguished by their strength and speed, artists by their creativity, scientists by their inventions and intellects, explorers by their courage, and educators by their moral attainments. Some women are praised for their beauty, while many others are clothed with prudence. Some nations are notable for their history, economy, and accomplishments. Some proudly narrate the Greek epics and ancient legends, while others share the Arabic suspended odes or the Muallaqat. Some talk about the pyramids and others about skyscrapers. We all look for distinctive traits that make us special in some way.

So I ask, how have you distinguished me and with what colours did you colour me? You empowered Solomon with wisdom, Job with patience, and Abraham with promises that continue to stir our memories. Hagar and Deborah's gift was a call to a celestial and victorious motherhood. Ruth is set apart by clinging to the God of Naomi and by living in the midst of God's people. But how do you set me apart and distinguish me?

My greatest distinction is that you listen to my prayers when I call out to you (v. 3). Your response drives away all worries and makes nagging inner complaints fly away. With my prayers I challenge evildoers and with them I comfort the upright. In prayer I discover the secrets of heaven and the faithfulness of the righteous Lord. The ship of my prayer crosses the roaring seas, plunges into the deep valleys between mountainous waves, but always comes safely to its moorings at the dock of good news.

The Lord hears the righteous ones and sets them apart. Ask and it shall be given, seek and you shall find. The Lord listens and grants peace and good sleep to all who lift up their prayers in the name of Christ. The Lord illuminates their hearts.

O Lord, today let us pull the ropes and let the bells of prayer ring. Selah!

~ Prayer from Psalm 5 ~

Judge them O God (v. 10). You are not a god who enjoys evil or overlooks the neglect of righteousness (v. 4). In your house there are no liars; they are not allowed to rent any space in your dwellings. You abhor shedding innocent blood, reject cheating, and hate crookedness (v. 6). You are perfect in holiness and righteousness.

You reject the arrogant, who hold their heads so high while their feet are rooted in lies and hypocrisy (vv. 5, 9). Yet while you hate, you also love! You abhor, but your heart is full of love! You judge and forgive. You confront people with holy judgment, yet you forgive those who fail in righteousness. How can you be the judge and simultaneously the helper of every sinner?

Like Spurgeon I ask, how should we as straw and combustible wood approach the eternal burning fire? With Paul, I cry out, "Are we any better than those who turned away from the right path, or those who are corrupt liars and full of envy?" (Rom 3:9–20). O God, you are the judge who will not stop condemning every sin, everywhere, and in every age. I lost my humanity as I drank from the cup of sin and got drunk with Satan. I am aware of truth and grace, yet I forgot the wisdom of heaven. Therefore in your court I am a guilty sinner.

What are the wages of such revolt and rebellion? David taught that sinners reap what they sow, but the Son of David paid the debts of sinners. On his cross, holiness and defilement met. The holiness of God and the defilement of humans came face to face. Justice and love embraced each other, and God embraced sinners. Indeed, you are the judge who judged all of us on the cross when you poured out your wrath on your beloved Son. The verdict is in, and I should be punished, but my Jesus paid it all. What a painful marvel! He tasted an eternity of hell and received infinite intense torture in a moment.

David discovered the richness of your mercy (v. 7), and on the cross of the Son of David we encounter your holiness and grace. You judged the wicked, and I am one of them. Then you punished our sin when Jesus dealt with our iniquities. You have destroyed our rebellion with his obedience. Therefore, I can rejoice in your holiness that does not accept sin. I delight in your abundant mercy to all creation. I celebrate the just decision of the heavenly court, and I am full of joy at the fullness of mercy that heals our wounds. It is through this mercy that I enter your house. I bask in your presence, in your holiness that is clothed with grace, and in the abundance of your mercy. Hallelujah! Holiness has become a source of comfort!

~ Prayer from Psalm 6 ~

The Lord has heard my cry (v. 8).

Jacob mourned for Joseph and refused to be comforted. Joseph must also have mourned the loss of his brothers while he was in a foreign land. To lose family members and those one loves is harsher than the lash of a whip.

Like Ezekiel and Peter I have sought the Lord with tears. Are my tears like the worthless tears of Esau? Or are they like the tears of Hagar when her son was almost dead? I cry like Hannah while I am praying and wishing for a different reality.

Ah, I am exhausted; my heart is full of fatigue and sadness. My body is weak and my spirit and soul are dwelling in darkness. O God, heal me. Have mercy on me, deliver me, and save me in my distress. Even my tears are tired. My worries are parked on my pillow, in a traffic jam of sorrows. How long O God (v. 3)?

Could it be that the Lord has forgotten? Has the flood of despair drowned the land? My courage has melted away and I can no longer cling to even a shred of hope.

But the Lord has heard my sobbing! He has gently wiped away my tears and granted me the desires of my heart. He has accepted me as I am, and in Christ I even bring him pleasure! Jesus wept and the chosen one cried out as for my sake he wrapped himself in pain. He was humbled for me. Then he became an intercessor at the right hand of God, transforming my tears into a plea that thunders in heaven. In the furnace of harsh realities, my tears have become like sand in an oyster; the Lord has transformed each of them into pearls. God turns them into a spring that quenches my thirst for a more mature faith.

O Lord, sanctify my tears on this day. Use them to bless your church and to help bring salvation to the world. I mourn in order that you may bring forth the dew and rain of blessings over our country. I sob knowing that you value and see every tear. Not one single tear will be lost. All of them will contribute to the spread of the kingdom of the master of the universe.

ᔓ Prayer from Psalm 7 ᔓ

O Lord, they accuse me viciously; they attack me with deadly words. They crush my reputation, gossiping about me without reason or substance. The tribe of Saul threaten me with their words and deeds. Remember Saul and his daughter Michal who despised the Lord's anointed one (2 Sam 6:16). Remember Shimei son of Gera who cursed him (2 Sam 16:5–14). Their words are daggers stabbing at our souls. The vulgar Sheba another aggressive Benjamite, joined them (2 Sam 20:1), and the list of liars grew as Cush the Benjamite joined in too (Psalm 7). They murder our souls with their words. They slaughter my name. I feel like a sheep struggling in the mouth of a hungry lion. They depict me as "Judah the traitor"; they are bent upon crucifying my name. So I cry out for vindication to the judge of heaven and earth.

You are the one who probes the hearts and the inner thoughts (v. 9). You are the one whose justice confronts the cutting tongues of slanderers. They bite and bark like dogs, but the Lord rescues those who are upright. Those who gloat shall not rejoice (v. 10) because God will speak while I am silent. He will stand up while I am sitting, and he will be exalted while I am kneeling.

He has prepared his sword, strung his arrows, and declared his holy war against those who filled their mouths with lies and against those who became experts in crookedness. Their minds are enslaved by false testimonies (v. 14). The liars are pregnant with disgrace. Their wombs are loaded with double-dealing. But they shall not give birth to such oppression. The Lord will lose patience and forbid it. They shall fall in the pits they have dug to snare others (vv. 15–16).

O Lord, I praise your holy name, for you probe souls to protect your children. You alone change this insanity, just as you converted Saul, grandchild of the Benjamites, into Paul, captivated by the love of Christ (Phil 3:5–11). Today, I trust that the Lord is my shield. He neither abandons the followers of Jesus, nor betrays them. O God, into your hands I submit my good name until the day of my death.

~ Prayer from Psalm 8 ~

O Lord, how marvellous is your name in all the earth (v. 1). I exalt, bless, honour, and praise you with every breath and every heartbeat. I praise you as I gaze into your heavens and galaxies, as I scroll through the pages of your universe in all directions. How great you are, and how wise! Elders exalt you and praise fills the mouths of newborns suckling and toddlers playing (v. 2). I sleep, but the stars continue to praise you. Then I wake up to see even the sun worshipping you and obeying your laws of creation.

You have given human beings dominion over creation, making me the master of mountains, seas, pools, and ponds. You have given men and women authority over the works of your hands and over every creature on earth (vv. 6–8). You have taught me to respect every human being and to deal gently with the elderly and the young. The lowest and most despised humans are greater than angels and every created light.

Christ honoured us when he clothed himself with humanity, and when he undressed us from death. You lionized us by giving us power. Then you increased our glory by the love you showed us on the cross, fountain of every blessing; the hill where you broke hatred's power. O death where is your sting? The Lord changes curses to blessings, diseases to healings, attacks to surrenders, contempt to admiration, and death to life. I may be insignificant in the eyes of evildoers, but not in the eyes of the all-comprehending Lord of the universe.

Today, I will honour every human being regardless of their religion, nationality, skin colour, age, or physical features. All are created in the image of God. The honour of God shall replace the contempt of men and women. O Lord how marvellous is your name in all the earth!

~ Prayer from Psalm 9 ~

L ord, you are a fortress for the oppressed, a stronghold in seasons of distress (v. 9). I praise you with all my heart, I exalt you loudly and sing hymns to your name, O Most High (vv. 1–2).

Enemies will fail, evil ones will perish for God is seated on his judgment seat. By faith I see that the enemy has been obliterated for all time (v. 6). The castles of Satan are made of sand; his evil snow has melted, and my Jesus has burst through the strongest gates of hell.

O Lord, you are my refuge when evil tribes attack me. You are my boat when the flood of hatred submerges me. You are my umbrella when the sky rains vicious words. You are my medicine when my tongue becomes sick, my mind crazy, and a devil sits on my chest. I forget, but you remind me. I fall, but you raise me up. I get hungry, but you fill me. I avoid you, but you pull me close to embrace me. I fear the evil ones and the uncertain road full of bumps and potholes, but you reassure me. You know everything and hold all living creatures in the palm of your hand. You are my refuge every day, in every season, and in all circumstances. You are with me whether I am strong or weak. You save me despite my betrayals. You are my eternal guarantor and the sponsor of your people and nation. You are good news to your children and a destructive tornado to your enemies.

Today, I shall stand outside the gates of death, the gates of destruction, hatred, oppression, and conspiracy. I shall sing, on that spot, to the Lord of heaven. By the grace of the Christ who has dominion over heaven and earth, I shall turn the gates of death into the gates of Zion, the sign of all signs.

~ Prayer from Psalm 10 ~

I have many enemies but I am not distressed, even if I encounter a hundred hardships. The problem neither lies in the conspiracies which surround me, nor in the insults of evildoers. My biggest problem is your disappearance and remoteness when I truly need you (v. 1).

We don't see God when we look around; we see conspiracies, lust, and blasphemies (v. 3). Christianity is dwindling. Instead of being called the land of blessings, curses dwell in our lands. Atheism is in Nazareth, along with corruption and false faiths. Evil spirits in Palestine, Israel, and the Arab countries have woken from their deep sleep. Knives of oppression cut up the land. It seems as if God does not care about the murder of children, the cheating of the innocent, and the spread of abuse.

Get up, God! Raise your hand! Do not forget poor men and needy women (v. 12). You are the parent to orphans, the supporter of the crushed, the giver of peace, and the one who spreads justice and security. Arise in the midst of your church. Arise in the lives of leaders as well as in the lives of little boys and girls. Rule over your church to outlaw struggle and division. Rule over our countries to banish harassment and killing. Listen to the groans of the meek and the weak. Let your Spirit pour out your gifts.

The solution is neither Islam nor money. My deepest desire is Jesus; he alone can quench our thirst. We want a king like Jesus to reign over us, correct our mistakes, and remedy our sins. O Lord, show yourself to your people in our country, churches, courts, streets, houses, and meetings. Today, you are the king of my life, my family, my church, my village, and my country. You are the authority over heaven, and earth belongs to you alone.

~ Prayer from Psalm 11 ~

O my soul! Escape to the bosom of God! Escaping to God is not cowardice. It is faith in the Most High.

Devilish arrows pursue me from hell, but they have no power to pierce the bosom of my Father. The wicked yearn to kill me, and to spill the blood of heavenly creatures. The world is in turmoil, but its destruction has no effect on the bosom of my Lord. The world's foundations are being overturned (v. 3), and goodness has become a deaf corpse. Yet, the fountain of love is still overflowing in the bosom of my Father. Oppression is as abundant as air. Distress and evil have become lovers. Yet, wide green pastures bloom in the bosom of my Father. Dragons of death surround me, yet they cannot scorch the bosom of my Father. There the sound of oppression is hushed. The threats of both the ignorant and the learned fade into the Lord's holy silence. Ignorant slogans vanish. The ink dries in oppressors' pens without a word being written. Love, justice, and peace dwell in the bosom of my Father. Light, rest, and security are found in the bosom of the Most High.

After burnout, breakdown, and blankness, it is glorious to rest in the bosom of my Father. There, rays of light illuminate my soul, and music quenches my thirst. I drink from the cup of faith, and I wrap my cold body in the warmth of peace that is found in my Father's bosom. I drink from the fountain of love and wear gentleness to meet my master.

What will every righteous person do in this season of betrayal and distress? What will we do when the wicked shoot from the shadows, and the foundations are overturned (vv. 2–3)? O Lord, I will recharge my batteries in the bosom of my Father. I will claim Christ as my centre and look into the face of my Father. I shall no longer see this world, but shall gaze into your all-knowing eyes. I trust in the Lord. May his glorious name be blessed!

⌐ Prayer from Psalm 12 ⌐

O Lord, what is shocking is not the extinction of dinosaurs and other animals; it is the disappearance of godly men and women (v. 1). Where are the godly heroes and heroines of the church? Where are the prophets and prophetesses? Where are those who raise the flag of love, justice, and unity? Where are those who store up treasures in heaven? Where are the ones who weep for the salvation of Jews and Muslims? What is the future of our children in these bad days, the days of evil? What is the destiny of my beloved ones in a land where Satan hypnotizes its people and puts them to sleep?

Instead of pursuing holiness and spiritual awakening, people are adopting the laws of the jungle. They lie, cheat, steal, commit adultery, and murder babies. Were their tongues created for lying, their lips for hypocrisy, and their heart for conspiracies? O Lord, who shall save the poor and miserable men and women (v. 5)? Who shall take care of my children and shepherd my little ones? I know that you will keep them safe and will guard them from villains and evildoers (vv. 7–8).

Today, I pray for my children. May Christ protect them and prevent the devil from hurting them through their friends! O Lord, teach them godliness. Teach them how to walk in line with heavenly realities in the midst of a hellish generation. Their world is violent and full of those who compete in becoming experts in evil. The Internet charms them swiftly into sin. They live in a world that has chosen "self" above God. Guard them, O Lord! And through them increase the godly ones in your church.

— Prayer from Psalm 13 —

O Lord, I am a prisoner of time. In a moment I was born, and I live my life moment by moment. Truly, all of my life is a mere moment. The past is a memory. The future is full of ambition, yet it is only a fleeting moment. All of my life is like a grain of salt in the sea of time.

It is a tasteless grain, for I live in a season of oblivion. God does not come to my celebrations. Worries and sadness invite themselves. Enmity and weakness continually stab my spirit. O Lord, does the sun forget to shine on us? Does water forget to quench our thirst? Do days forget to spin the wheel of time? Does gravity forget to pull its strings? Do songs forget their melodies or food its taste? How, O Lord, could my soul forget you? How could my heart forget to pulse your rhythm? How did sadness become my companion waking and sleeping? I get up and sadness sips coffee with me. I sleep and it shares my pillow. This sadness not only has a bad temper, but it also brings with it disturbing friends: worry, misery, laziness, and apathy. It lives inside and feeds on fright, fear, and despair.

I shall divorce sadness. I shall wash the dirt of gloom and worry from my face. I have decided to meet you with a plea. Don't hide your face from me. Every day, I shall beg at your door for a crumb of grace and a sip of joy. I shall smother my sadness. I shall strangle my worry, trusting and believing in my Lord. I shall sing to the Lord for he has blessed me. He has delivered me from the prison of time. He freed me from the fear of days and reminded me of the meaning of his great presence. The Lord of eternity shall shatter these shackles of time. This illusion of days will be blown away like clouds dispersed by the light of heaven. I trust in the mercy of God, and my heart rejoices in his salvation. I shall sing unto the Lord who is the reason for my joy and freedom

～ Prayer from Psalm 14 ～

O Lord, when I watch the ignorant I see thoughtlessness spouting out of their mouths, and I see their dirty deeds (v. 1). They shut their eyes to your glory in heaven, your work in history, and your millions of acts of love. They say that there is no God. They walk away from the divine Christ. There are so many ignorant people in our times; our country is filled with them!

Is there anyone who understands and who seeks God (v. 2)? They have all turned away from paths of decency and rejected good traditions. The goal of their lives is first to eat and then to spread corruption on earth. They fill their bellies with pleasures; they devour everything to please themselves. They consume your people with their sharp teeth and spit out Christ.

What is the worth of religion without Christ? What is the value of drums without heavenly rhythms and celestial melodies? Prayers are worthless without the blessings of heaven, without holy altar coals. How widespread is ignorance these days? How countless the stupidities? There are many who pray believing only in themselves; religious men and women as well as atheists. There are those who worship humanity and good social standards. What shall I say about those who run after cash and thrills, who spend their lives in contemplation of their bank accounts? What shall I say about those obsessed with appearance, sex, carnality, assaulting God with their indignity? Is there anyone who understands and who seeks God?

We have forgotten that you love mercy, justice, truth, love, and self-sacrifice. We have murdered orphans and stolen from those who have nothing. We oppress ourselves with apathy and laziness. Strangely, we continued offering our prayers despite the blood on our hands.

O God of truth and grace, restore us from exile. Deliver us from the ignorance of our times and turn us into a people of understanding. O Lord, root me today in your understanding, in your heart, and in your divine will. Let me reflect you in my daily actions and reactions.

～ Prayer from Psalm 15 ～

O Lord, how can I find you? Who dwells with you? Numberless Muslims worship in a mosque in Jerusalem, more than numberless in Mecca. Jews are still praying at the Western Wall. Hindus are washing themselves in the Ganges, while Buddhists honour Buddha and fly to his country. Sikhs are celebrating in India. Across the world, all of us are looking for a home, for a divine nest for our souls. How can I find you and where do you dwell? Where is the nest of my spirit?

The problem is not in the location; it is in the seeker and the one who has the question. The answer is not found on the map, but it is connected to the heart. Before I find the answer to the question, I myself need to be the dwelling. God's house is in his people. The address is within the son of Adam and the daughter of Eve.

But how do we find a son of Adam who is always truthful and perfect (vv. 2–5), rooted in a righteousness unshaken by season or circumstances (v. 5)? Who can go through the furnace of God's holiness and sit in God's bosom? Who can live a heavenly life in the land of men and women? Will I not find God before finding this man? Without him I shall not be able to find the nest of my soul or leave the land of sorrows.

But praise God. God is Spirit and Jesus Christ is the revealed heavenly map. God and humanity meet in him. Joy and sadness meet in him. The longings of the spirit are fulfilled in him, and we find our home and security in him. On this day, I come to Jesus and follow him everywhere. I worship God in every place and at all times.

Prayer from Psalm 16

O God, how great thou art! You are holding my future in your steady hand; you are my portion and destiny. It does not matter what kind of ministry I have, for my reward is you.

My accomplishments and victories are not my concern. I yearn to be under your protection and care, and in fellowship with you. When you are my portion then I am a winner, and my reward is the greatest prize. When I am in your hands then I am at the centre of your will. O my soul, let the Lord be your counsellor (v. 7).

I shall declare that you are my leader who walks before me. Then I will reap blessings and will not be shaken (v. 8). I will rejoice, exult, and be comforted (v. 9) for I trust that you are my deliverer (v. 10). I shall know the paths of life and experience the overflowing of pleasures and blessings that you intended for me (v. 11).

O Lord, if you walk before me that means I follow you. There are many who follow other people and other gods (v. 4) and as a result their pain multiplied. But I, O Lord, shall walk behind you and follow you wherever you go. You are the fountain of blessings and the refuge of humanity. You are pure goodness, and there is none apart from you (v. 1).

— Prayer from Psalm 17 —

O Lord, someone said to me, "If your prayer can't ignite people's hearts, how can it possibly ignite and stir the heart of God?" That is true. If I have no conviction, how can I convince you? David prayed fervently. Thus, he was able to convince heaven and earth.

In this psalm, I discover that your eyes probe our hearts before listening to our prayers (v. 2). You keep us protected under the shadow of your wings when evil attacks (v. 8). Thus, we need to fix our eyes on your face (v. 15). Then we shall become undefeated heroes who continually conquer evil and multitudes of evildoers.

David prayed with lips without malice (v. 1) and with an uncomplaining heart (v. 3). His life and behaviour were pure before the Lord. It is thus important for us to fast, to be sanctified, to purify our hearts, and to love God sincerely with words and deeds. Then we pray in truth and faith, and we seek God's protection from oppressors who spread violence instead of justice (vv. 9–10).

My prayer today is prompted by a world full of evil and violence. O Lord! Keep me as close as the pupil of your eye, cover me with the shadow of your wings, and hide me from evildoers (v. 9). I shall keep my gaze fixed on your face in the midst of hardship and danger. Instead of letting fear paint its image on my face, I shall look like you (v. 15).

Either we look at the faces of evildoers or at the face of God. Either our faces become horrified and full of gloom, or we become like God. O Lord, may my face become like a mirror that reflects your truth and peace!

~ Prayer from Psalm 18 ~

O Lord, my life is a minefield, but you are my strength (v. 1). You are my boat upon the floodwater of fear. You are my shield against death-dealers and demons (vv. 4–5).

When I am distressed, weakened, and impotent to change my reality, I shall throw myself on you. I shall knock at your door seeking to encounter the King of heaven and earth. You are the King of kings, the strongest person, and the most glorious being. You burst out of your house to protect me and fight evildoers (vv. 6–16). How powerful you are against their puny fists (v. 17)!

I don't care about their high positions or their deadly weapons, for you are a circular wall around me. With you on my side, I shall face all evildoers (v. 29). You are my support in the midst of dangers. You are my helper today, tomorrow, and the day after tomorrow. You protect me here, there and everywhere. You are my shield whether I am prepared or at my weakest. I praise you O Lord on this day. I love you O Lord, my strength.

~ Prayer from Psalm 19 ~

Heavens, earth, and all of creation testify that you are the greatest being. I ponder your colourful, lazy lilies of the field; they grow without labour or spinning, yet full of beauty. I contemplate your birds of the air, sowing nothing, harvesting nothing, yet replete with your generous gifts. Then I look at the ant and consider its ways. I recognize that you are wise, and your wisdom is seen even in the smallest creatures. You have made all of your work in wisdom. You have given your creation life and blessings. You have opened your hands to satisfy us with goodness. All creatures long for you because you are the centre of the universe. The planets, suns, comets, and galaxies don't move without your permission. I have heard that the sun stopped once at your command; the stars danced to the melody of your plan. They led the magi to your bosom.

O Lord, today I shall look at the trees, the birds, heaven, earth, and all of my surroundings in order to bless you. I shall praise you, magnify your name, describe your superiority, and highlight your unique abilities. I thank you, because you have called me to live in your exhibition. You are the greatest artist in the heavens and on earth. All of creation is your exhibition.

Your glorious creation is a blessing to those who follow you as well as to those who hate you, but your new creation is only for those who understand that you are the greatest artist. You are the sculptor who can turn earthly humans into heavenly ones. You can turn the image of corruption into incorruption. O Lord, my life needs a painter that can re-draw it and reform it. Knead me, crush me, and form me. The outcome will be a masterpiece that is suitable for heaven because you are its creator.

～ Prayer from Psalm 20 ～

O Lord, I cry out to you on the day of my distress (v. 1). It is a day that is full of challenges and limitations. On this day, I discover that I cannot handle all of my problems. My resources and experience are not enough. I have tried. I decided to change things, but I did not prevail. I truly need a saviour.

There is no saviour better than you. You are the greatest and most compassionate saviour. Therefore, I will not invest my efforts and energy in recruiting the resources that people use to address their problems. Instead, I will start with something unique and come to you. Some trust in guns and tanks, but we trust in the name of the Lord (v. 7). In my distress, my life will be different; my thoughts, feelings, and decisions will be different; for I shall come to you and trust in you. I shall trust from the bottom of my heart that the outcome with you is very different.

You alone are God and we are the children of the blessing. Our King is not deaf or harsh or impotent. I thank you because you have entered into the day of distress and turned it into a day of supplication (vv. 1, 9). You have blessed me in the midst of my distress and consequently my inner soul has recognized that you are trustworthy (v. 6). I surrender my life into the hands of the one who can calm waves and dry tears.

～ Prayer from Psalm 21 ～

O Lord, may the rulers rejoice in your strength and salvation (v. 1). I pray for the leaders of the Middle East. Do not give them hearts of steel like the hard heart of Pharaoh who refused to show any mercy. He did not listen to the voice of God. Do not make our leaders like the militant Nebuchadnezzar, who strove to conquer and exploit others. Instead, make them like Cyrus, whom you called the anointed one of God (Isa 45:1).

May our leaders be your servants (Rom 13:4) and then our servants! Grant them your eternal blessings and reveal to them your salvation (v. 1). Answer their good prayers and let their hearts rejoice in you; let their faith in you grow (v. 2). Prevent the devil from controlling their hearts, lest they carry the flag of death. Instead, change the hearts of our leaders; convince them to create civilizations of love and life, rather than regimes of hate or death. Fill them with your blessings (v. 3), lest they become a channel of curse.

Make them a blessing to those inside and outside your church (v. 6). May they bless every poor, widowed, and needy person, and all those who are in pain! O Lord, dissolve the thick glue that keeps them on their tyrant thrones. May they instead stick with you, with truth, with mercy, and with justice, so that our countries can live in tranquillity, quietness, godliness, and honour (1 Tim 2:2)! O Lord, bless the leaders of the Middle East in the name of Jesus Christ. Amen.

~ Prayer from Psalm 22 ~

O Lord, why have you forsaken me? I am a Palestinian, a Syrian, an Egyptian, and a resident of Gaza. Why have you forsaken me (v. 1)? After sunset, darkness prevails. There is no rain; drought is everywhere.

I look at the symptoms trying to discern the disease. As I contemplate my predicament, I wonder if you have forsaken me. Where are your first mercies? Where are the spiritual awakenings and the blessings? I pray and you don't respond (v. 2). Do you consider me your son? If so, why am I considered a disgrace before the world (v. 6)? Your church is dispersed and on the run in Iran, Syria, and Iraq – so many places. I have nothing to be proud of; I feel like a despicable worm before the rest of humanity (v. 6). I have no beauty in me and no fortitude.

I am surrounded by evildoers trying to kill my Christian faith and my religion (vv. 12–18). Extremists kidnap your followers in Syria. They threaten us in Egypt. They kill us in Iran. They write hate language against us in Israel, and they terrify us in Gaza.

Ah Lord, may your sun rise again on the Middle East! Deliver us from the mouth of the lion. I want a divine revival! Will you not bless our countries?

Yes, you will bless us in the name of Jesus. I shall tell my brothers and sisters that you are coming and that you are the blessing itself. I shall tell them that you have not hidden your face from us. You shall continue to see and to listen because you are just. I shall tell them that all the ends of the earth will come back to you, and all the tribes of the nations will kneel down before you. This is your assured promise.

Ah Lord, I wait for your healing. Come and heal our country from this epidemic. Come, O Lord Jesus to Bethlehem, to Jerusalem, to Nazareth, to Tel Aviv, to Syria, Lebanon, Jordan, Egypt, and to all the countries of our region. May every knee bow down before you! Honour your church in the Middle East. We want a whole nation to be born by your miraculous work. We want a nation that worships you because it has recognized that Christ is alive! O Lord, may this future shape my present!

∽ Prayer from Psalm 23 ∽

O Lord, you are the shepherd of my life. You shepherd me. Therefore, I shall not need anything, whether I am in good pastures, or in the valley of the shadow of death, or even sitting across from my foes. I shall not need anything whether I am in health and strength or on my deathbed. You satisfy all of my hunger.

Whether I rest safely in good pastures, walk in dangerous valleys, or sit in the presence of enemies, you are my assurance. You are my guarantee and my insurance even if my bank account is small or my sickness fatal. You are the shepherd who does not have hungry sheep because you are always full of blessings. You restore the lost soul and calm the troubled heart. You never abandon your lost sheep or those in peril from evildoers or wolves. I sense your presence in the good pasture, but I feel your tangible presence in the valley of the shadow of death where you show me extra mercy.

You have even revealed your rod and staff to tell me that you are with me. Like other sheep, I have discovered that the shadow of the dog cannot bite! The shadow of the sword cannot cut! The shadow of death cannot destroy me! Your sun shines in the strangest places! Whenever dangers increase and hardships multiply, you reveal yourself in the most tangible ways. Now I am sitting across from my persecutor, but you have honoured me with miraculous protection.

You have arranged your table with a wise plan and revealed that you satisfy your people not only in the good pasture but everywhere, in every season. Even when I become a fleeing refugee you are my refuge. You welcome me to your table. You are the secret of my contentment despite my circumstances. Today I seek you, for I know that with you every goodness and mercy is always present. Into your hands I submit my day, O Shepherd of my life.

~ Prayer from Psalm 24 ~

O Lord, I thank you for the important questions in my life. You ask, "Who may ascend the mountain of the Lord? Who is the King of glory?" You are looking for a different kind of hero. Most heroes play mind games or enter contests judged by beauty, speed, or strength. But your heroes and heroines are the champions of love, kindness, and repentance. They surpass others in humility, generosity, righteousness, godliness, and commitment to the unity of the church. They are committed to loving the poor, the needy, the refugee, and the prisoner.

Who can win the contest of the Lord? Who can be a hero or a heroine today? Who can go up to the mountain of the Lord? You challenge me to new purity of thought, word, and deed. You challenge us to be upright, to become godly men and virtuous women. You challenge me to be a saint every moment of every day. You challenge me to be a spiritual hero and a legend in goodness.

Psalm 15 presents this challenge to all people, but all of us have failed. Humanity has failed. That was why the beloved John wept and wept in Revelation 5:4, for no one was worthy. No, I am not perfect. I am lost and I am a sinner. I can't meet your standard of perfect love or purity of heart.

But you can still make a hero out of me. Because you are the King of glory, you can re-create me as a hero. Who is this King of glory? He alone is the one who can open the eternal gates: the gates of heaven, the doors of holiness, love, and divine strength. He can open the gates of Zion, the city of God. He alone is the key to the coming of the kingdom of heaven on earth. By his grace, I can enter into his presence. By his strength, he keeps me pure and turns me from a sinner into a saint. He turns me from Esau into Jacob, and from a child of wrath into a child of grace. I shall become one of the people of God, chosen in Christ. He is the King of glory who will let me enter the city of glory!

Yes, I will be a spiritual hero or heroine today. I can do all things in Christ who strengthens me; in Christ . . . in Christ . . . in Christ. Hallelujah!

~ Prayer from Psalm 25 ~

O Lord, yesterday when I read Psalm 24, you asked me, "Who may ascend the mountain of the Lord?" Today, you ask me another question, "Who is the person who fears the Lord?" (v. 12).

I always look for answers and forget the significance of a good question. I forget the importance of the journey in which you shape my life. I look for learning and forget my teacher. Perhaps I don't want to live in a puzzle and prefer a pleasant life without painful valleys or difficult mountains.

But, O Lord, you are not asking me a question so that I might answer it. Instead, your question breeds a set of questions that test my heart. In this acrostic psalm, I am reminded that the person who fears the Lord is every man and woman who trusts in you and waits upon the mercy that flows from your hands. It is the person who discovers the mercies of God and his goodness after a long wait.

I shall not become a person who fears God if I don't first discover that I am the chief of sinners. John Bunyan understood that his sins were greater than those of David, Solomon, and Peter, for he denied the risen Lord and abandoned the triune God. I shall not really fear God unless I discover the scope of the damage my sin has caused to your heart. I need to discover this, and hate what I have done!

Augustine says that the depth of my sin is related to the scope of the damage it causes. Its punishment is proportional to its damage, not to its frequency or to the amount of time invested in it. My sin has wounded God, killed the Son of God, and insulted the Holy Spirit.

But you are a good lord (v. 8), a teacher of righteousness (v. 9), merciful (v. 10), and a forgiver of our sins (v. 11). You have disclosed your heart to me. Yes, I fear God; therefore I won't run away from him in panic, but will run to him with a loving heart. I fear God; therefore, I shall not become terrified and full of anxiety but will sit next to the cross, the fountain of my beloved's love where my thirst is quenched. There I drink forgiveness, strength, and grace. To become God-fearing, I must stay close to worshipping Christ every day.

O Lord, turn me into one who fears God. I willingly come to you to form me, to shape me, and to help me to walk in your convoy day by day. Turn me into someone who fears but does not flee! I want the fear of God to dwell in me so that I honour and magnify you in my heart, in every decision, and in every action every day.

Prayer from Psalm 26

Vindicate me, O God (v. 1). It has been said that there is no forgiveness without punishment because God is just and sin must be punished. Either this punishment comes upon me or upon Christ who died on the cross in my place. Either I represent myself, or I accept that Christ represents me, but punishment is on its way. And when I forgive the sins of others, I do it to honour Christ who paid the penalty for their sins and mine. I thank you, O Lord, because your justice is the foundation of your forgiveness. Without the justice of the cross, there is no divine forgiveness. Justice and forgiveness cannot be divorced.

But, O Lord, I live in a world without justice, a world full of bribes and favouritism in employment and in providing services. I have no tusks and claws, but I am surrounded by people in high positions with teeth like swords and tongues that sting like scorpions. They are like flies that suck my blood. There is no justice in our world, and there are no just people. Instead, we have tyrannical states and oppressive laws, and the strong are like a pack of wolves hunting down newborn lambs.

Vindicate me, O Lord. I will not stab people in the back. I am not going to allow my anger to boil up into grudges and bitterness. I am not going to twist my tongue to flatter power. Instead, I shall direct my prayer to you, O just God. Purify my heart and have mercy on me. Empower me to invest all of my efforts in looking up to you rather than down on my enemies. Empower me to sit with you and praise you instead of standing among warring people. Let me meditate on your wonders instead of talking about the oppressive behaviour of evildoers.

I hate strife, arguments, bribes, and vice. Don't surround me with soul murderers but with humble people who offer themselves on your altar. I shall bless the just Lord who will not leave the poor abandoned, the refugee ignored, the prisoner destroyed, or the oppressed crushed. He will not leave the oppressor free, the exploiter victorious, or the liar at the front of the line.

You, O Lord, are just. The sun of your justice dawns on the face of Christ. I see its beautiful rays and am waiting for its everlasting noon. I shall raise today the flag of your justice. You are the highest judge, and I rest my case, as well as my struggles, in your hands. I lay my life within your fists. I accept your decisions and celebrate your sovereignty. Please Lord, so fill my heart with righteousness that I am a channel of your justice and not a dam that prevents the flow of your kingdom.

⁓ Prayer from Psalm 27 ⁓

O Lord! What shall I do on the day of evil that David mentions (v. 5)? On the day of evil, Eve deceived Adam, Cain killed his brother, and Jacob's children sold their brother Joseph, the beloved child. On this day, David looked at the wife of another and was defeated by lust, and evil-doers put Daniel in the lion's den. On this day, Job lost his beloved and pain became his companion. On the day of evil, the wicked attacked the baby Jesus and killed all the young children. Sinners crucified the Lord of glory, and the rivers of hell overflowed their banks. On the day of evil, they killed Stephen and Antipas, imprisoned Peter, and lashed Paul. On that day, nations were dispersed and wars spread. On the day of evil, hell attacked earth; devils celebrated an orgy of death.

What shall I do on the day of evil when evildoers approach me (v. 2) and Satan spreads his army around me (v. 3)? What shall I do when my closest friends abandon me, and even my father and mother run from me (v. 10)? As I confront the tragedies of this life, my heart is becoming hard like stone.

What shall I do when this tornado of darkness swirls over me? Shall I not cry out with David, "You are my light and salvation therefore I shall not fear." You are the refuge of my life therefore I shall not be horrified (v. 1). You hide me in the warmth of your bosom and transform the day of evil into one of goodness. Your grace flows through Moses' staff and turns my stony heart into a spring of mercy, grace, holiness, and righteousness. The wolves around me are transformed into sheep that follow you.

You alone conquer evil and turn the curse of the cross, along with all its darkness, into the eagle of righteousness that carries the blessings of heaven in the folds of its wings. You are my light, never extinguished, however deep the darkness. You are my salvation, never withdrawn, regardless of the many enemies of peace.

I shall enter into your presence, where worry and despair disappear. I shall throw myself into your hands where evil flees. Light will dawn in my heart, bringing peace and tranquillity, despite the darkness. Your grace saved me yesterday. Your grace keeps me safe today. Your grace will be with me tomorrow and until the day of my death. I worship you on this very day and trust in you.

~ Prayer from Psalm 28 ~

O Lord, I call to you for help (v. 2). Do not turn a deaf ear to me (v. 1). Do not be silent. I cry out to you with holy feelings. I call to you for help. Don't break my heart. Don't close your ears to my cry for help. I need to hear your voice and guidance.

Don't close your mouth, O Lord of words. In one utterance you created the sea; with one word you fixed its limits. With one word you calmed its roaring waves, and with one utterance you split it like you did at the Red Sea. You commanded and it was so! I call to you for help! Please speak to me!

Your silence is torture. It is worse than wandering in the desert. Without the light of your Word, my darkness will not be driven away, my tears will not dry, and my country cannot be healed. Your silence is a bitter cold and I am naked. Wrap me with your Word. Your silence is my painful hunger. It is like a burning hell. Help me, help me! Please, please, speak.

Listen to my request and speak your word of truth and justice. Speak in this country that is full of evildoers. They worship day and night, but heartlessly and unlovingly. I live in a country full of peace plans and friendly speeches, but war and treachery lie between the lines. Evil dwells in people's words. These same people have crucified your Word, muzzled it, stabbed it, distorted it, and killed it. But it still speaks. It rises from its grave and raises all of our country with it. All nations shall be silent before your Word's podium.

Your resurrected Word will remove the bitterness, anger, and murder that lie like a boulder blocking the entrance of our souls' tomb. With your Word, life, truth, mercy, and love shall rise. Speak, O Lord, for the sake of our country! Kill our country's evil with your Word.

Blessed is the Lord, for he is the hearer of prayers. Indeed, the Word spoke, became human and lived among us. But his people still need ears to hear. So Lord, give us ears. Create in us the same ability to listen that was found in Samuel. He said, "Speak Lord, for your servant is listening."

So, speak Lord when I open my mouth; speak when we love and cry. On this day, turn your church into the most beautiful sermon known to human beings. Turn her into a discourse of love and life directed to a world full of hatred and death. O Lord, speak on this day for I am listening. Speak through me and honour my tongue by making it a messenger with a heavenly message. Save your people, bless your inheritance, shepherd them, and carry them in the name of Jesus Christ.

∽ Prayer from Psalm 29 ∽

O Lord, I believed you were wordless. Then I found that the problem does not lie in your clear voice but in my dull ears. It is not the broadcast but the reception that is faulty. Indeed, the voice of my brother Abel is still screaming, but I don't hear because my heart won't listen. Moses spoke, but I am a deaf Pharaoh. The voice of the Lord is still calling even in our day saying, "Samuel, Samuel!" But our Samuel is asleep and can't hear. Perhaps Eli is still telling us, "Go back to your bed and your comfort."

O God, you have made the heavens to send messages and the stars to offer proclamation. They testify that human beings and all of creation are made by God. Even the mouth of babes and sucklings utter wisdom, but I don't hear it. The birds twittered, the storms came, fires spread, and the rain poured down, but I did not have ears to hear. I saw you hungry, begging at the roadside, but I did not hear. You were sick and distressed sitting in an alley, but I did not listen. How can you heal my ears from apathy?

You meant it when you said, "Whoever has ears, let them hear." You even became human; the Word spoke in our midst. The voice of the Lord was present in every street and neighbourhood. Even if humankind is silent, the stones cry out!

Please open my ears to hear your story; the great creation story witnessed by heaven, the great redemption story testified by myriads of mouths. You are not a silent God, but my ears don't work properly. Will you unblock them? Make them hear your heartbeats and longings. Open them to your voice, your guidance, and your discipline. I pray that my ears may become larger and my hearing more mature. Then I shall become the person who hears the voice of God every day, everywhere, and in everything.

Prayer from Psalm 30

O Lord, you turned my wailing into dancing (v. 11). You entered my life and redeemed it from hell. You then closed the gates of hell in my life and put out its fires. I magnify you every morning and every evening. I was sick, but you healed me. I was perverse, but you corrected me. I was deceived, but you guided me. I was a prisoner, and you freed me. I was surrounded by wrath, but you were pleased to grant me life. I thank you, praise you, and exalt you. My spirit sings for you. My life was like a dark evening, but because of you, it has become a rising sun. I exalt you because you are the sun of goodness in my evenings and mornings.

In the midst of my pain, my eyes poured out tears, but you wiped them away. Ah, Lord! Thank you for bringing me back. I am at home and at rest in your loving bosom.

Don't abandon the one-eyed and lame, for I am one-eyed and lame in my spirit. I shall approach your throne, for you are the healer of both body and spirit. I shall worship you, for you are the one who removes my pain and pulls me up from my muddy pit. This day is a day of thankfulness and praise. I thank you wholeheartedly. You are my hero, and I trust in you.

Prayer from Psalm 31

O Lord, deliver me (v. 1). O my rock, refuge, and shelter, save me (v. 2). My eyes are consumed with intense grief; deep sadness is over me (v. 10). My bones are corroded; I am an object of repulsion to all my foes; I have become like a destroyed pot (v. 12). But my life is in your hands (v. 15). I am sick and my body is tired. My throat is dry because of bitter humility. Weakness and sadness clothe my life, and my tongue is constantly complaining in the midst of temptations.

I have become weak, and I have groaned, but I have also prayed, asking you to take away my sickness and sadness. Take all weakness away from me. Do I need a divine paddle in order to leave this sea of sickness? Will my shoulders be strong enough to paddle on in the face of such storms?

Death stopped at my door with a drawn sword. He was accompanied by Worry and his friend Fear. O Lord, remember that my soul is in covenant with you. You alone are my shield, and I am but a grain of sand hiding inside a seashell. Into your hands, I commit my fatigue and disease.

Before your eyes, I am like transparent glass. You look into my inner soul, but because of your grace, I am no longer scared. Shine with your sun on my darkness, and bring your life to my feebleness. Make my praises and singing like that of the birds. Fill me with grace, healing, and sensitivity to heavenly realities.

I thank you! You, the greatest potter, can re-create my heart. I trust you today, knowing that you listen, see, and judge with justice. Remove my humiliation and restore to me the joy of praise, whether I am here with my people or there with my ancestors.

⁓ Prayer from Psalm 32 ⁓

I confess to you my sins. I don't hide them. I admit that I have betrayed your covenant and that my sick heart is full of bitterness. I wish that I had kept the laws of God and had been sensitive to the promptings of heaven. Instead, I killed holiness itself; I spilled the blood of love and truth. I have done evil in its fullness. When I stand before the mirror of truth, my iniquity is clear and cannot be hidden.

But your hand of purity touched my defilement; the light of your love dispelled my fear. You have redeemed me with a young ram. Therefore, praise dwells with me instead of guilt; mercy instead of torture. The Lord removed my falling tears and freed a hostage from the grip of Satan. He changed my life and distanced me from Satan, the liar and cheater.

Why am I like a dumb mule that keeps forgetting the laws of forgiveness? My deeds are not the means for forgiveness, and human food will not satisfy the hunger of my spirit. Nothing will keep my spirit from being famished except the bread of the Most High. All the bakeries and cookies of hell will fail.

O Lord, wash me with the blood of the slaughtered lamb and feed me from its meat so that I can get rid of my shameful iniquity. Make the sun of holiness rise on the land of sin and remove all my germs and dirt. You are the omniscient physician who knows the secret depths.

O Lord, I thank you for your forgiveness. On this day, I put all of my iniquities before the cross of the greatest being. I shall be a debtor to your grace for the rest of my life, and you will be the giver. On this day I am mindful of every sinner and traitor. May you turn their eyes to the cross and to the Christ who is sovereign over all villages and cities! May crowds of Arabs approach the fountain of forgiveness, by land as well as by sea!

～ Prayer from Psalm 33 ～

O my soul, come and let us shout unto the Lord! Let us pray. Let us praise and sing! Let us magnify his name with strings. Let us exalt and praise the name of the Lord. May we increase our praises! God is good, faithful, and righteous. We shall encounter his mercy wherever we look or walk.

With one word, he created the world. He commanded, and his word was obeyed. Before the power of his word, our ability to explain disappears. We cannot describe the impact of his words, but our minds are drawn to kneel down in worship.

Millions of people fight against God without fearing or magnifying him. They don't recognize that the secret of life is in the grip of my King. The secrets of blessings and the treasures of grace ride on a word from his mouth. Blessings and miracles are in his hands, as well as the best future for my child and my country. He is the Maker of the earth, of family, of sons and daughters. He is the creator of all. At all times, he is the most honest hero of love, even in seasons of betrayal and fatigue. His eye is on those who fear him and who hope in his mercy. In death, he delivers us. In the midst of hunger, he grants life. What a marvellous king is God!

People choose the best to be their king, but a human king depends on human provisions, and therefore he fails. But I trust in the Lord who saves and delivers. What a great joy for me to be the bride of the divine King! I wait for the knight of my salvation, who is my stronghold and shield. I trust him and wait for a soft comforting touch from his hand. He alone is the owner of my heart, and to him alone I covenant my life. I am yours, O my King. This is the day of the Lord! Rejoice my soul and sing.

～ Prayer from Psalm 34 ～

I bless the Lord at all times (v. 1). I depend on him because he is my helper. I was afraid and he rescued me (v. 4). In my distress, I cried out and he heard me (v. 6). I was hungry and he fed me; he treated me better than even lions (v. 10). I was alone and he embraced me, and by the angel of the Lord, he delivered me (v. 7). I was insulted but he honoured me (v. 5). I shall honour the Lord who granted me insight when I looked up to him. I cried out and he listened. I was hungry, but I am now satisfied by the comfort of the Lord. I asked, and he answered me.

O Lord, you see all of my life and all of my needs. You see my desires and inner thoughts. You see my fears and anxieties. You see the visible and the invisible. You know all of my secrets. You hear all my groans and listen to all my music. Where are Beethoven and Mozart to play my praises? Without Jesus, their best melodies are worthless. You hear the strings of my heart and the drums of my spirit. You hear the rhythm of my thoughts and dreams. You hear the melodies of my silence more than my words. My body, soul, and spirit play in the orchestra of my prayers. Jesus, my Christ, is leading the singing. The Holy Spirit is providing the melodies. Hallelujah!

You are the food for my spirit. You arrange before me a table, and my soul drinks from your cup. The thirst of my spirit is quenched. Behold the dish of peace next to the dish of joy; love is the centrepiece of my redeemer's table. Behold the tree of life and the heavenly manna, as well as all the delicacies for which my spirit longs. Behold and taste how good is the Lord (v. 8). He is the passionate love of my spirit. I bless and praise the Lord. Today is a day of praise. Hallelujah!

~ Prayer from Psalm 35 ~

O Lord, there are too many battles going on around me (vv. 1–4). I find myself facing not just one Goliath, but an army of Goliaths! I keep meeting people who are like the Amalekites. They make me feel so small, like an insect, and as insignificant as a bread crumb.

Instead of there being just one Judas, a whole nation is becoming like Judas. Its people are experts in treason. They have stolen our land, killed my dream, and displaced our boys and girls. They are like a waterfall of fatigue and a flood of bitterness. I am exhausted from fighting devilish men and women.

I call upon you today, asking you to fight on my behalf and to end my groaning. Fight evil with my tongue and destroy bitterness with my deeds. May the storm of love come and the tempest of grace approach like a strong wind! Then evil shall fly away and curses shall be driven away. May the angel of the Lord defeat and expel the evildoers (v. 5)! Let the angels sing the most beautiful melodies!

O God, come and reveal the eternal power of the cross and change the life of Goliath. Turn him into a David, just as you did with Saul whom you turned into Paul. Paul's life overflowed with divine grace. O God, you are the wonderful warrior who not only fights hellish people but also protects heavenly ones. You send the light of Christ to break Satan's covenant with his hellish followers. You free and justify us. You deliver and save us. Your salvation is tastier than a delicious banquet!

Some have done evil for evildoers. Some have done good things for righteous people. But I will do good deeds even for evil men and women. I shall be sad if their souls perish, and I shall add my tears to theirs, pleading for the victory of good in them. O my Christ! Fight on my behalf. You are my hero, and only your presence can guarantee my victory and a life full of miracles.

All my bones cry out, "Who is like you?" My mind is captivated with your exaltation and praise. O fountain of my righteousness and hero of my battles, may all people exalt you! In the midst of division, you peacefully encountered enmity and strife. They hated you for no reason. Yet you loved them and used their hate to heal their souls. You healed them from worshipping themselves. They hated you and sent you to the cross. It is marvellous that on the same cross, you destroyed their hatred with love and miraculous affection! Divine blessings overflowed and countered all the curses. Your blessing won. Today, I don't ask you to destroy all the enemies of God but to remove Goliath from their hearts. Turn every Goliath into a David after your own heart.

~ Prayer from Psalm 36 ~

My generation is no longer wise (v. 3) and my people have abandoned doing good deeds. My countrymen shout in the streets, and their cars carry loads of iniquity to every mountain and valley. The darkness of night is in control and iniquity dominates my day. Iniquity controls my night and the darkness of Satan sits on my bed. I carry the sins of my country on my shoulders. Ah, I am so tired. I am a killer, a thief, a blood spiller, a liar, a worshipper of money and false gods, a blasphemer, a hater, and a person with malice. I am against even myself.

Today, I shall stand before the creator who judges the whole world. Woe be to my country, for sadness is the portion of my people. Words are no longer able to speak, and I am completely paralyzed. Divine justice demands that my country be disciplined; its destiny is prison, flogging, and pain. We have killed the Son of God and rejected the Messiah of our salvation. Ah, O Lord! Have mercy on my country! Do not destroy my home! I stand with Moses. With Ezra I intercede, and I cry with Paul, as I reflect on the failure of my people and my country. We are without Christ and without God.

O Lord, come to every sinner and call them. You have been, are, and always will be the merciful one (vv. 5, 7). Will you not quench the thirst of my country and give it a drink from the cup of celestial blessings (v. 8)? Will you not enlighten my people in the midst of their darkness, and provide a fountain of salvation that quenches the thirst of my life (v. 9)? Have mercy, O God, and save my country. Didn't Jesus cry for Jerusalem? Are not his tears interceding for my country too?

O darkness of my country! I rebuke you in the name of the crucified Lamb of God. He is the hero of love and the fountain of miracles. He is my Lord and my God. My iniquities and the sins of humanity buried him, but he rose from the dead! By his resurrection, the church shall rise along with heavenly dreams. The Lord shall end the exile of my country.

~ Prayer from Psalm 37 ~

Delight in the Lord, and he will grant you the desires of your heart (v. 4). Trust in him and he will not disappoint your trust. O Lord, I shall act faithfully and nourish faithfulness, for this is the path of your children (v. 3).

But the man who plots evil has found me, and he desires to steal the peace you granted me. He embraces wickedness. His path involves enmity towards your followers. Yet you instruct us to be patient and not to fret over his success (v. 7). You tell us to refrain from anger (v. 8). Your statutes command us not to embrace evil as we embrace our loved ones.

O Lord, how shall I delight in you and how shall my life be in union with you? Help me to see that my life is a drop in the seas of your eternity, but it is a drop that is in the grip of your hand! The secret of tranquillity is surrendering to you and fulfilling your dreams.

O Lord, my weakness is a spark that you can fan into the flames of your victory. My despair is the gateway of your hope. My failure is the bridge to your success in me. Therefore, I shall stop delighting in myself and discover your peace. I shall not follow the path of Adam by trying to replace you with me. Life is not about me in your earth or heaven; it is about your place, your name, and your dreams.

I shall stop thinking about the delights of my soul and my weakness, and instead be busy delighting in you. What do you think and how do you feel? I want to be in your bosom. Where do you move and work? What is your latest painting? Tell me about your strength, kindness, and beauty. I have forgotten the desires of my heart because I am caught up in your thoughts, grace, and celestial delights. I have forgotten my dreams and anxieties before the beauty of your vision and dreams. I have forgotten my tears as I listen to your laughter and see your joy. Without your touch, my reality is mere imagination. You are life, and I shall not find any peace before I discover your peace.

O Lord, I delight in you. This is not my day, but your day.

～ Prayer from Psalm 38 ～

Your arrows are embedded within me, and your hand weighs heavily on me (v. 2). There is no sound spot in my flesh, and there is nothing healthy in my bones (v. 3). Ah! My sins, my iniquities have piled up over my head like a flood that smothers me (v. 4). My guilt is too heavy for my back, its pain too strong for my body. It cuts my spirit. I have spoken as if I am an enemy of God and think like a devil.

Therefore, God disciplined me. His hand came down upon me. My hips are burning with pain (v. 7), my wounds are in flames. Even worse, my spirit is bleeding and burnt out, all because I acted in stupidity (v. 5). I groan from the beating of my heart, and my moaning is before you (v. 8). I am at the lowest point; I am completely exhausted and the light of my eyes is no longer with me (v. 10). All the ships have sunk, and I am drowning in the sea of my despair. All my friends and loved ones have departed, while my enemies have multiplied (vv. 11–12).

O Lord my God, would you answer someone like me? I have sinned against you in word and in deed and in apathy. I acknowledge my soul's treachery, and I do not hide my iniquity. Your punishment is just. The suffering of my soul is deserved. I am deeply distressed because of my sin (v. 18). I have gone astray and sinned against you. Before your court I have no defence or argument.

Is there any hope for someone like me? Diseases multiply in my body, and weakness of spirit is burning within me. Ah, O Lord! Grant me a drop of mercy. This is my request. Wet my spirit with one drop and grant me a moment of compassion in the midst of this fire. I have never forgotten your love and kindness. Your salvation has always been on my mind. I have nothing. Even in my best moments, there is nothing I can offer to compensate for my corruption. You have no reason to keep me alive. You have every reason to kill me and finish my life. But now I submit my life into the hand that has stricken me, knowing that it is also a merciful hand. I plead for mercy, knowing that the one who wounds can also bandage my wounds.

In Jesus I find my deliverance, for your hand came down upon him in order to save me. I cast my cares, fatigue, and sickness on him, and I trust in his salvation. O Lord, don't just accept my corruption; grant me deliverance. Accept me in Jesus, for in him lies mercy and healing for my wounds. May I be accepted in your sight! May I not be the target of your deadly arrows!

~ Prayer from Psalm 39 ~

O Lord! I am ephemeral (v. 4). My days are short, less than a few minutes long (v. 5). My life is like straw in a fire. It is like a breath, an illusion, a brief sunbeam passing through the dense clouds of time.

Why do I forget that my days are like a drop of water in a hot frying pan? Why do I forget that all the treasures of earth will be left behind? I am a grain of sand in the desert of this life. I am like a forgotten thought and a thread that burned in the fire of time. My life is like a bird's dive in the river and the jump of a fish in the air. All of my life passes in a second. All of my potential and position are dust. I appear for a moment; then I am gone.

I do not want to think of death, but it thinks of me. I do not want to go to death, but it comes to me. It carries with it important wisdom: I am ephemeral. Therefore, I shall put a muzzle on my mouth (v. 1). I shall drive away the love of money from my heart. I shall remember that I am a stranger and a sojourner like all of my ancestors (v. 12).

What is the hope of human beings in the land of time? What is the lasting treasure, and what is the healing hope? What is the most important thing in a life that lasts only one moment, a moment that is full of worry and anxiety? You, O Lord, are the only eternal being who can protect us from death. You are my hope (v. 7).

In you time stops and a breath becomes an eternal moment. A moment becomes a gateway to a river of days. My life is but a moment of pain, but it is followed by a full heavenly life. It is a moment of termination, followed by hours of bells of glorification.

Life does not equal happiness, but life with God is full of joy. Death does not equal misery, but death without God is eternal damnation.

Even if all of my life is but a moment, I shall spend it with you and in your pleasure. May my life become a moment of prayer, a moment of light when God shines through me into the darkness of this world! May this moment be a breath of mercy and a sheltering shadow for the wretched! May this moment be a cry of truth and a tear that mourns for the sake of those I love! May it be a drop of divine water in the furnace of time and a breeze of cold air before the flames of the wrath! May my life be a moment of divine love to every person! Only this kind of life makes the moment worthy of living.

～ Prayer from Psalm 40 ～

O Lord, my heart is full of trouble, and evil is more numerous than the hairs of my head (v. 12). A friend reminded me that I can no longer do what I have to do, or what I want to do, or what I used to do. Where is courage and affectionate spirituality? My spirit's medals of honour are burned. I am now in the pit of destruction. I am in Satan's land, where forgetfulness dwells and my soul fails.

I wait patiently for the God of my soul (v. 1). He turned to me from a distance in order to hear my groaning; in the midst of my turmoil he established my feet (v. 2). The singing of my spirit returned, along with my laughter (v. 3). Your word pierced my ears and dwelt in my inner parts (vv. 6–8). Your word is so gentle especially when it touches my wounds. Your whisper is like curative oil for my wounded spirit. It is the best wine. It is the best music for love and a party for my spirit. My Lord shall save me and take care of me. He is my helper and deliverer (v. 17). Can the celebration of my hero, who will not accept my destruction, start now?

I shall drown my tears in the words of God and then wash away my worries. I have waited so long, and my heart is sick, but it is impossible for my God to fail. I shall put on the garment of praise and fill my mind with prayers. I shall prepare the depths of my soul with obedience to my God's statutes. I shall make myself beautiful and stand before my groom. Then I shall call him to dwell with my spirit. Your word lives in my womb and my mind. Your dreams are the map of my path and I long for your presence in me. Your presence is the peak of my joy. The table is set; come, O my most precious one! I have arranged the table and my spirit is waiting. I wait for you today. Don't be slow, O my Lord!

~ Prayer from Psalm 41 ~

O Lord, I don't want to think about it, but it thinks about me. I don't want to go to it, but it comes to me. Good health will not stop it. Youth, strength, money, dominion, and power will not stop it. It knocks on my door. Then it slaps me in the face with sickness. It ties me to my bed with weakness (v. 3).

Then it starts preparing its feast of celebration. It wants to suck out every breath of life and kill my soul. A choir of evil accompanies it. Their hellish melodies numb my connection to you. Their song is "When shall he die? When shall his name be obliterated?" (v. 5). Their chorus is, "He slept and shall not rise again" (v. 8).

People told me there was an angel of death, and behold, I am encountering an army of death-angels. I meet them in sickness, in the midst of my iniquities, in my enemies, and in those who hate me. All want to hurt me (v. 7). All belong to an evil conspiracy against me (v. 5). Even my closest friends conspire against me (v. 9). They have betrayed my covenant and shackled death to my hands and feet. The same one who shared my bread paved the way for death to come. He was supposed to be my close friend (v. 9)! But he signed a contract to hurt me; with his dirty foot he stepped on me.

O God, have mercy on me. You alone can keep me and bring me back to life (v. 2). You are the eternal God. Have mercy on me. Don't leave me, but face death instead of me. Fight my war. Heal my sickness and terminate my death. Frighten the powers of evil, destruction, hatred, hurt, treachery, weakness, sickness, iniquity, and every evil spirit that has plunged its teeth into me. Free me; make my ears deaf to the songs of evil. May my death die and my life rise in its place!

Ah, O Lord! Although I can't escape death, I shall exult with praise in the face of my enemy. Jesus is alive, so death will not overpower me. O Lord, my feet shall stand in your presence forever, and then I shall bow down and worship. Amen and Amen!

⟋ Prayer from Psalm 42 ⟍

O God, as the deer pants for brooks of water, so my soul pants for you (v. 1). Why, my soul, are you downcast? Why are you so disquieted within me (vv. 5, 11)? O Lord, why? Why do I forget your strength? Why do I forget the labour of your love? Why does your absence distress me? Why is my soul cast down when you depart?

Away from your bosom, my soul is like a withering flower. It is like a dry land, far from your streams of water. No other kind of water can take your place. The waters of the Nile are polluted with blood; the waters of Marah are bitter (Exod 15:23). Like Naaman, I have considered the rivers of Abana, Pharpar, and Damascus. But your purity and blessings are not found there. I have drunk the waters of both mountains and valleys, but my spirit is still thirsty for your pure water and your days.

My tears are my only drink, day and night. Instead of your words, I encounter insults. There is no more water in my waterskin. Like Hagar, I need your guidance (Gen 21). Like David, I long for a glass of water from your home (1 Chr 11:17). Like the Samaritan woman, I stand before a deep well without a bucket that can reach to your soul. Like the deer that pants for streams of water, I long for your touch.

You sent Rebekah, and she gave my spirit a drink. Then she gave a drink to my camels. At a well, I met Rachel, and she was kind to me. Moses drank, and he let others drink – that too was by your sovereign grace. But well water is not enough. I must go back to your land!

O Lord, do not forget the refugees, those with heavy burdens, and those who seek your peace. From the abundance of your grace, let all who are thirsty drink. In your presence may the water be mingled with the Holy Spirit! Then we will not only hear your sermon to Nicodemus, but like the Samaritan woman, we will also experience water overflowing in us.

May your water quench the thirst of humanity and restore us to your path. Your word is true: Jesus is the straight path and the one who can quench the thirst of our souls. In him I quench my thirst and find your presence.

~ Prayer from Psalm 43 ~

Why, O my soul, are you downcast? Why so disquieted within me (v. 5)?

O Lord, plead my cause against an unmerciful nation (v. 1). My ancestors lost their homes, my parents lost their dignity, and my children are losing their future because evil is begetting evil. It is continuously pregnant with hellish evildoers.

Anger begot wars, and exploitation nursed abuse. Children's books teach hatred and provoke them to kill. Now their eyes are able to hunt at night. Our children have grown up, and human beings are becoming monsters. Oppression is their meal and their path is complete destruction.

The excuses that spread bitterness are endless. In the name of a country's security, and even in the name of God, they have made a huge prison. They have locked up the children of God. Security has become their religion and their golden calf. Its altars spread wide to extend violence. Security is a false prophet who spreads lies. Its helper is a vast wall, a merciless pile of rocks. The people have raged and stormed, but the current laws uproot their lives like trees. Security has spread the religion of Cain and the logic of continually stepping on the neck and corpse of a brother. Evil has imprisoned our hearts. Its walls have become our home. Therefore, our souls are downcast, and our tears are shedding even more painful tears. Our story is the story of the failure of humanity to show mercy. We all lack love, mercy, and understanding.

O Lord, will you not come back to end our exile? Won't your truth come to destroy the altars of false security and fatal hope? Won't your light come to illuminate our path? You are our hope and glory, especially when human beings are acting like monsters. Shine with your light and presence. Create a new humanity. Create a new future that reverses all previous fortunes and injustices. May peace flow like a river in our country! May love and justice become the path for all the inhabitants!

We intercede today for the oppressed and the downcast. O Lord, free them from hell, hellish people, and multitudes of violent demons.

~ Prayer from Psalm 44 ~

O Lord, it is not my bow that I trust; it is not my sword that will save me (v. 6). The enemy have opened fire with machine guns filled with bullets of hate, and evil has filled their television screens. They are targeting my country with bombs, missiles, and wars. Hellish people have put off love and crucified grace. Death is painting obscene art in which terrorists pull out the eyes of young children and rape women. Revenge has become a desirable pleasure.

My people, my family, and my heart are wounded, murdered, and dead. I am reminded of Moses, who interceded before an angry God, pleading that the flock of the Lord would not become extinct. With Abraham, I am stunned, for I see that the righteous are among the dead in Sodom and Gomorrah! They are in the graves of evildoers! Will the Judge of the Earth not do justice? Won't he prevent the destruction that pelts us, like driven sleet? Doesn't the whole Middle East have even ten godly sheep? Won't you show mercy to Nineveh, with its tens of thousands of people?

We have not forgotten your covenant, and you are aware of the secret thoughts of our hearts (vv. 17–21). Won't you have compassion on the church of Christ and hear our prayers? For the sake of your name, we have been like sheep led to the slaughter. We are slain every day, and death consumes us (v. 22). Yet death is still hungry, and it destroys the boys and girls of the Lord of heaven. Why do you allow children to be kidnapped and increase our humiliation? Please make the disgrace of your church a memory! Please start a series of miracles today! Wicked people are active, and hellish forces are rising. Where is the God of love, redemption, and abundance of mercy? Don't hide your face from the cry of Palestine, Lebanon, Syria, Egypt, Tunisia, and Sudan. Listen to our prayers. Remove our disgrace and restore your glory and pleasure.

I cry with Paul when I remember that you did not have compassion for your own Son, but turned him into your greatest gift! At the bottom of the sea of hardships, you have planted a seed of life and victory. Therefore, I shall wait for your mercy when the sun of your compassion rises. Nothing shall separate us from the Lord of heaven! Please send your help and make the necessary changes, for you are the one who hears our prayers and groanings.

~ Prayer from Psalm 45 ~

My Master, you are the fairest of all human beings (v. 1). Your throne lasts forever and ever (v. 6). Your beauty is the desire of all nations. Heavens seek to praise you, and all nations worship you (v. 17). You are mighty in love, and your grace captivates our imaginations. Justice, mercy, and truth are all your ways. There is none like you!

In your presence, words flood my heart, and my tongue is transformed into the stylus of a prolific scribe. The giants in my life become dwarfs, because I have seen your glory. My fear becomes a joke, because I inhale your perfume. As a result of a mere glance full of love, I gladly choose to become your bride. Every desire of my heart dies, except the desire to seek your face. I forget every perfume except the fragrance of your clothes and the joy with which God your father has anointed you (v. 7). With all of my heart, my behaviour, and decisions, I love you.

You take pleasure in love; therefore, I adorn myself with your love. Wearing embroidered clothes woven with threads of holiness, mercy, and covenant, I enter your palace.

Let the whole world hear about the love and praise of your church. Let them contemplate her beauty and glory, and your fascination with her. Every groaning or pain in the name of God is a perfume or ornament with which we adorn ourselves for you. We forgive and pardon. We show mercy and love. Then we love again and again as we adorn ourselves for you!

Those who don't see your bride's beauty are blinded by Satan and cannot see you. Those who muddy your bride encroach on your glory. But yet I am beautiful because of you. O love of my life, come and make my heart your home.

～ Prayer from Psalm 46 ～

O Lord, you are the one who can end all wars (v. 9). You are our helper in the midst of hardship and suffering (v. 1). Even if the mountains stumble into the heart of the seas, our hearts are fearless in your presence. The tsunami of murder and criminal acts shall not drown the God of Jacob. You will build your church, and the gates of hell will be knocked down before your army.

Wars are followed by more wars. We all struggle with evil and bigotry. We continually flee from hatred. Bullets fly around us in every direction. Syria, Palestine, Egypt, and other nations groan. America, Europe, and the United Nations cannot prevent the madness of wars. Therefore it is time for you to release the armies of peace from the multinational church. Let the sun of the city of God rise and turn the noon of evil into a sunset.

Like Francis of Assisi, I pray that wherever there is hatred, I may be able to sow love and declare every human being beloved. Help us to spread peace where there is strife and division. Where there is abuse, let us spread forgiveness and eclipse the power of hatred. Where there are lies, let us spread truth and declare that Satan is going to be defeated. Where there is despair, may I plant seeds of joy in the land of gloom. I want to comfort before I am comforted, to understand before I am understood, to love before I am loved, and in the season of war, I pray that I am a drink of peace.

May my life become a bridge for peace and a mirror reflecting the beloved Son and Prince of Peace! May my life become a battleground for fighting against hatred and oppression! May I become an oasis for the oppressed and exploited! O Lord of Peace! Be exalted in the nations for your name is awesome. May all wars die! May your grace overflow in your church! May it empower peacemakers to go out to the whole world!

~ Prayer from Psalm 47 ~

O Lord! You are King over the whole earth (v. 7). You are a great King and the Lord over all nations. You are the highest ruler in every country. You are the one who can calm all revolutions (v. 3).

You have given us hands to clap with joy for you. You have given us voices to pray and shout in jubilation (v. 1). Palestine and Israel sing! Jordan prays to God. All the nations unite in worshipping you. O children, praise the Lord! O men, proclaim that the whole earth belongs to God. Let the girls and women praise the Lord. Let the nations walk in truth and justice. Let their praises become deafening. Let the people of Abraham and the dignitaries among the nations praise together the King and Lord of the whole earth (v. 9).

The Most High rules; there shall be no more division and war. God has commanded the blind to see, the crippled to walk, and the deaf to hear. As he commanded, it was so. Lazarus rose from his grave; therefore Mary and her sister rejoice.

O music, play your melodies for the King of the earth is bringing healing! He is the healer. Let the countries of the world be filled with churches that praise in spirit and in truth. Let Arabs and Jews pause to recognize that the whole earth and all who are in it belong to the Lord. Instead of searching for who owns the land, let us fill our countries with justice and love, and let us clothe our countries with praise that begets holiness. Then all the walls will fall, and strife will end. All wars will cease through the church's miraculous praise and worship. We will sing of peace, unity, and love. Our lives will sing mercy to the whole earth and its creatures.

By his crucifixion and resurrection, the King of kings sat on his throne judging the nations. People of God, sing praises, for such singing heals the sickness of our earth.

O Lord! Turn my day into a song of praise that makes my people rise from the dead and be restored to their God. You alone are the legitimate King and owner of the earth and all its inhabitants. Today, I shall sing unto the Lord who has dominion over the whole earth.

～ Prayer from Psalm 48 ～

O Lord, kings gathered and conspired against Zion (v. 4). They mockingly said: "Let us attack the city of God." They scorned the house of God and despised his people. They desired to control Zion, the joy of all the earth (v. 2). They wanted to exploit and destroy without any consideration of the God of all gods. They did not see the pillar of fire and the righteous angels. They did not ponder the height of Zion and her God. Can a straw fight fire? Can a grain of sand fight a storm? They did not consider God.

O people of God! Believe, and you shall be secure; trust and you shall succeed (2 Chr 20:20). Don't be surprised when God builds Zion, which is the mother of all of us who are free. Remember that Zion was betrothed to God on the cross. Be mindful that he loves her and gave his only begotten Son for her.

Her castles are made of grace; sinners take refuge in her. Many generations meet in Zion to testify to the blessings of the Most High and to praise him (v. 13). Ponder its towers that point to the miracles of God. Egypt, Assyria, Babylon, and Rome were humiliated before Zion. Every tower reminds us of the blood of the saints and their faithfulness. Consider these towers. Then consider that we shall not be overcome by fear! We will not kneel down before threats.

Consider and stop your attacks. Zion's temple is the desire of heaven and earth. It is the fountain of mercy, so consider and seek mercy. Many enemies have drunk from the mercy and grace of this fountain, and then they have encountered the pleasures of God.

I love you, O church of the Most High. You drive out demons by the finger of God. All the ends of the earth are mesmerized by your beauty. O Lord! Bless your church and help her boys and girls to understand that in Christ they are more than conquerors. May the presence of the Lord fill us today! May your people rejoice in their unity in Zion! May evildoers see your grace and strength, and be so terrified of evil, that they flee from it (vv. 4–6). On this day, we bless the church, our mother, and pray for her in the name of Jesus.

~ Prayer from Psalm 49 ~

O Lord! I have seen death with my own eyes. It destroys the strength of the powerful and demolishes the wealth of the rich. It confuses us all. It treats the rich and the poor equally (v. 2). It deals in the same way with the old, the young, the generous, the stingy, the fool, and the wise (v. 10). But this equality fades when we evaluate things from the perspective of wisdom. Only then do we see the comfort of Lazarus and the torture of the rich.

In death we see the end of the world and the futility of every desire. O death, I stare in your face! Such glances make me ready to be received without shame by my God. O death! My mind relishes the thought of death every day because I trust in God alone.

At the moment of my death, I shall be like Jacob and bless the Most High. I shall instruct my family and tribe to do what is good. Like Aaron, I shall take off the clothes of my ministry and appoint the person who comes after me. Like Moses and Joshua, I shall affirm and encourage my people, pouring out my heart before them. Like David, I shall be concerned about the house of God before you take me, remembering the blessings, the person, and works of my God. I shall count the Lord's blessings in my house and in the paths of my life. Like Stephen, I shall grant forgiveness to everyone around me, far and near.

I am not afraid now, for God has redeemed my soul (v. 15). His seal of life is engraved on my heart. The king of horror cannot consume my spirit, for the King of life has redeemed my body, soul, and spirit. He conquered death with his death, and he forgave my sins. And now I am like Penuel's daughter (Luke 2:36–38), worshipping with prayer and fasting until I see you, my Saviour. Bless me like Simeon (Luke 2:25) so that I won't see death before I see my Messiah and Lord.

Like Paul, I know that the crown of righteousness and the blessing of faith are both waiting for me. My time has come, and I am confident in the Most High.

～ Prayer from Psalm 50 ～

O Lord of Justice! Turn me into a prophet in an age full of terrorism. Martin Luther King said, "Injustice anywhere is a threat to justice everywhere." Therefore, I shout, "O people, who forget God (v. 22), listen to the Lord of lords!"

There are countries full of hungry children, while other countries' stores are filled with dog food. There are patriarchal societies where women are in bondage and where sex trafficking is spreading. Some invent weapons of murder and destruction. Others find silly excuses to continue to use those weapons. Oppression muzzles truth. The strong blindfold the weak and hinder the mobility of the oppressed. They close the borders, as well as the doors of opportunity. Sometimes they do it in the name of security or politics, while at other times in the name of protecting their loved ones. They legalize stealing from the wretchedly poor and allow violence to spread without reason.

Their deeds will not intercede for them. Their "good" works are futile because their religion is void of compassion and justice. It spreads hatred and destruction. Their offerings and sacrifices will be rejected because God can see that inside they are like wolves.

Let us instead protect the weak, feed the hungry, and care for abandoned widows and orphans. Let us challenge oppression and be mindful that we are but dust. God does not need our sacrifices, offerings, or vows. Remember, he is the creator and giver of all (vv. 7–14). Without justice, all our offerings are futile, and our deeds are like a mirage.

Sacrifice unto the Lord with praise, and make justice your path. Then you shall see the salvation of the Father. May we spread righteousness and justice with the wisdom of the old and the strength of the young! Let us make the lives of the heavily burdened easier. Let us follow Jesus, the Lord of lords, and bring the good news to the poor, heal the broken-hearted, and release the prisoners. O Lord, make me a prophet in an age of wickedness and terrorism.

~ Prayer from Psalm 51 ~

O God! Have mercy on me and wipe away my iniquities (v. 1). My heart is defiled; please create a pure heart within me (v. 10). I forgot the letters and words of righteousness. Would you please fill my lips with your praise (v. 15)? I am humiliated by my iniquities. Sin has conquered me and defiled every speck of holiness in me. It is declaring its lordship over all of me. Every moment it has controlled me, even when I was in the womb of my mother (vv. 3, 5). My hands are cuffed with transgression. My feet have slipped and fallen deep into the mud of sin. I am overwhelmed by sin from head to toe. Dirt has crept into my heart and mind. Defilement dwells in my soul.

O God, wash me of my iniquities and cleanse me from my sin! I plead that you will have mercy on me! I seek your forgiveness; forgive me! I desire your compassion; have compassion on me! I am in Christ, begging for your approval. Accept me! Free me, and I shall be free. Justify me, and I shall be justified. Come to me with your salvation.

You are a just God, but don't give up on me. Don't cast me away or strike me. Have compassion on me. Restore my heart and my love. Accept my broken heart and the spirit within me. I deserve nothing, but in the name of Jesus, please do good to me. O Lord! Have mercy and wipe away my iniquities. Let your Spirit dwell in me and renew me. Let your blessings flow in me again. O Lord! You are the God of second chances, but I can't try again unless you first begin your work in me.

O Lord! Have mercy!

~ Prayer from Psalm 52 ~

O Lord! There are so many mass murderers and dictators. Stalin, Lenin, and Hitler are still alive. Pharaoh and Herod are still busy murdering people. They have united in killing Arabs. One dictator makes millions fear; how much more we fear as we encounter an army of dictators!

Doeg has joined them; he is a wicked servant of Saul and he hates upright people. He wants to hunt the anointed ones of the Lord. He is indifferent to Ahimelech and other believers. He joins those who spill innocent blood in the name of politics and religion.

We all identify with the son of Jesse, for our necks are under the sword of the Benjamites. They have killed the priests of Nob and only Abiathar is left.

How horrible are the wicked! They have become experts in spilling blood. They love evil more than good and deceit more than truth (v. 3). They love war more than peace and hatred more than love. They love uncleanness more than purity and ugliness more than beauty. They prefer turmoil over tranquillity. They spread hunger and oppression instead of satisfaction and vindication. They love Satan more than God and death more than life. They prefer to spread sickness rather than healing. They are monsters in the form of human beings. They have become rich by impoverishing others and have increased their strength by devaluing others.

O Lord, may the flags of dictators fall and the rule of criminals be terminated! May the age of infanticide, rape, exploiting minorities and the weak, expire! Won't you pluck the destructive forces from the land of the living (v. 5)? They worship their wealth and strength. They exult in corruption; they attack God and his people without fear (v. 7). Let them be recreated; grant them a new birth in order to make them blessed. As for me, I am a green olive tree in the house of the most merciful. I trust in God and hope in the Lord who is sovereign over the whole world (v. 9).

~ Prayer from Psalm 53 ~

O Lord! People seek science – they even travel to faraway China to learn more about it. They constantly long for more money. They lust for beauty, spending hours before the mirror. But they do not seek the Lord. Instead, they prefer to be without any lord.

They turn human beings into apes and declare biblical stories fables. Materialism and suspicion are the path of the agnostic. They live as if, "There is no God (v. 1); there is no judgment after death." They despise the miracles of God and argue, "Why should we help the poor? Why should we assist others?" Instead of learning the logic of sacrifice and doing good, they argue that it is more beneficial to be idle and corrupt. There is no creator of the universe; therefore the religion of Darwin advocates the victory of the strong over the weak. Distorted science might lead to atheism, but wisdom leads to God.

Some deny God in their minds; others deny God in their behaviour. Both are atheists. They devour the people of God with fingers that drip with sin (v. 4). Atheism is like giving a hungry person a toothpick; there is no way it will satisfy their hunger! Eyeglasses don't help because atheists have been blinded by demons; nor are their philosophies helpful. They argue that religion is the opium of the nations, but it is their spirits that have been drugged with lies.

O Lord! I call out to you today in the presence of many atheists. I am a disciple of grace and love; I carry the flag of the God of the best thinkers, the one who is the most merciful. I used to think that if I acquired the strength of God I could change the world and its inhabitants; but if I acquire both the strength of God and his wisdom, then I shall understand and accept the plan of God.

O Lord! I pray for the spread of the kingdom of the God who is sovereign over the whole world. The ignorant cannot deny the existence of the sun by closing the curtains. They cannot deny the existence of air by holding their breath. That is false logic. Blindness does not prove that light doesn't exist. That is the logic of hell.

When the sun rises, I not only discover that it exists, but by its rays I also discover the whole world. I know that I am not a coincidence. I am not a mistake. I am not an ape but a beloved son of Christ, the faithful redeemer who died for me. O Lord! I humble myself before you as I pray that you will restore the captives. O Lord! Restore the captive atheists and agnostics and turn them into Christians (v. 6).

~ Prayer from Psalm 54 ~

O Lord, "Grant me the serenity to accept the things I cannot change, courage to change the things I can, and wisdom to know the difference" (Niebuhr). I do good deeds, Father, but in return, people do evil to me. I have saved the city of Keilah (1 Sam 23:1–13), but they delivered me to Saul. So I escaped to Ziph, but many conspired to kill me. I had the power to hurt those who fought against me. But I chose to submit to God, who judged between us. To grant pardon when I can is the righteous path.

O Lord! I accept that you save me and shepherd me (v. 1). I accept that I cannot change my circumstances and life-seasons. I have no ability or artistic capability to do miracles. Before dozens of events, I pray proclaiming my need for a rescuer. And I declare that you are my saviour and shepherd. Encourage me to allow you to change me. Encourage me to raise the white flag declaring my surrender to you. Help me to fight my instability and win my war by putting you before me (vv. 3–4). Help me to face Amalekites in the name of my God, to encounter Goliath in faith, and to confidently walk on the water in the midst of the storm.

Like Mordecai and Daniel, I shall not bow down except to God. Courage is not the absence of fear, but conquering it in the name of God. It is not the absence of risk; it is offering my spirit on the altar of my God. I shall not discover the seas of God if I stay on the shores of my dreams. I shall not discover the Lamb of God unless I offer my Isaac on the altar of my surrender. I would rather live one day as a lion of God than live a whole life as a faithless coward.

When I sit, I consider you and surrender to you. When I walk, I encourage my soul with your wisdom and praise you with song. May this day be a day of courage in the name of my God!

~ Prayer from Psalm 55 ~

Cast your burden on the Lord, and he will take care of you (v. 22). Pray for your enemy, and the Lord will protect you (vv. 16–18). O Lord, how beautiful are your promises! But without your presence my life is a horror movie. I am confused, afraid, terrified, and in turmoil. Fear tears my heart, and destruction dominates me (vv. 2–5). How can I escape and avoid destruction? I wish that I had the wings of a bird to escape this dark storm of evil (vv. 7–8). I wish that my distress was a dream and that I would wake up from this nightmare!

I pray that I may no longer walk in utter darkness. May the seven cords of evil: violence, strife, iniquity, distress, corruption, oppression, and deceit (vv. 10–11), collapse in your land and country! May my heart be healed from the wounds of betrayal caused by my close friend! He was the twin of my spirit and my close companion; we knocked at your doors together (vv. 14–15). O Lord! I expect evil from my enemies, but my pain greatly intensified when Judah was born in the house of your beloved ones. He broke the covenant and destroyed our agreement. I thought that he was your friend. His talk was smoother than butter, his words more soothing than oil, but his intentions were like a fatal sword (v. 21). He stabbed me in the back, but the greatest wound was to my spirit, for the bite of the wolf cannot be healed without your cure. I would have preferred to meet a roaring lion rather than to be stabbed in the back by the companion of your children, my brother!

But I trust in God and cast my burdens on him. I know that you will take care of your children today. This is your credible promise, and I trust in your word.

～ Prayer from Psalm 56 ～

O Lord! I depend on you; therefore I shall not fear (vv. 4, 11). I trust in you; therefore I have courage and praise you like Asaph. I trust in you; therefore I walk upright in cities and villages. Like David who stood before Goliath, Elijah who stood before Ahab, and Hezekiah who stood before Sennacharib, I trust in you. And I learn from my ancestors. What can I say when I see the trust of Ezra, Nehemiah and Esther, who made you their cover and refuge? I trust in you, for you can see even a black ant on a black rock in a black night.

You heal us from the sins of our fathers and from ancestral drunkenness. You help those who are staggered by evil to be alert. Therefore I, by trusting you, lift up my head in villages and cities. You teach me continually so I am not afraid. I know that you are always able; therefore I shall not be afraid.

Evildoers persistently seek to destroy my peace (v. 2). My tears are before you like restless messengers (v. 8). I trust in you in my distress, for I am one of your sheep. I trust in you, who can split the seas, withhold rain, and control the rivers. You are my refuge in the storm. You command a fish and it swallows Jonah. You control the worm as well as the pumpkin to fulfil your goals.

I thought that if I were omnipotent like God, I could change many things, many outcomes and consequences. Then I realized that if I were truly omnipotent and full of wisdom like you, I would leave things the way they are, without any addition or change. I totally trust in you, for you are wise without limit, all-knowing, strong, insightful, merciful and faithful.

I shall not fear. I trust in you because you love me, and your cross is the signature of your covenant with me. You will never abandon me, even in the midst of our strife. I know that your presence is my greatest guarantee, for as long as you are with me, even the sharpest sword and most skilled attacker will never hurt me (vv. 1–2).

~ Prayer from Psalm 57 ~

O Lord! I am your church who takes refuge under your wings (v. 1). Hold me close to you, like the pupil of your eye. You alone are my helper. My soul is cornered by hungry young lions (v. 4) and the hunter's trap squeezes my head. Many put snares in my path, but I cling to your wings and fly over the circumstances of my life.

They killed the prophets and stoned the missionaries. Won't you gather your chicks under your wings like a hen? Hide me under your wings so I can't see the evil outside and can be comforted by your warmth. Like a suckling baby, I nuzzle into your wing, but you are both my father and mother! I bury my head in your wing and disappear into your inner feathers. There I listen to your heartbeat and tune the strings of my heart to harmonize my life's melodies with yours.

I cannot protect myself, but I can be protected in you. The frostbite of sin is painful, but the warmth of your wings is my refuge. Under your wings is not only a hiding place, but also my dwelling place. It is not just a place to visit or a site for tourists, it is my home! There I shall praise and sing. There my heart is steadfast (v. 7) and I raise my head confidently over my enemies. There I can see the cherubim, the ark of the covenant, and the holy of holies. There I see the mercy seat and the blood of the redeemer. There I am able to observe earth from heaven's perspective. There I can watch your mercy rise up as high as the clouds (v. 10), and you lift me up with it. Then my fear becomes so small and my worries insignificant. Under your wings is the holy of holies. There I see the end of evil, and I am able to relax. There my energy is refilled, refreshed, and you fill my life with the fuel of heaven.

Under your wings I discover your amazing greatness and sing unto you. My inner peace is able to bloom and flourish. May my every moment and heartbeat be under the wings of my God!

～ Prayer from Psalm 58 ～

O Lord! Truth is silent, and lying is the main speaker (vv. 1–2). Wisdom is deaf, but ignorance lends an ear (v. 4). Justice is blind, but oppression has eyes! The standards are confusing! I live in an age when judges are becoming monsters. Religions are becoming swords on our necks. Judges, journalists, and international councils have turned us into sheep and themselves into hungry lions (v. 6). We cry out, but they don't listen, for their standards are full of oppression, corruption, and evil (v. 2). We bleed, but they don't bind our wounds; they think of us as mice. They are like hungry snakes ignoring the painful cries of the poor (v. 4).

May evil fail and its arrows fall to the ground (v. 7). May its ability and influence shrink like a melting snail (v. 8). May the devices and plans of evil crumble (v. 9). May their conspiracies fall from the womb (v. 8). Evildoers have become active enemies of the kingdom of God. Satan himself has appeared in their midst. He has empowered corrupt oppressors to prepare a cross for our Messiah.

David is praying and we join him, identifying with his words of judgment and vindication, as we do with our Messiah. In this psalm, the church speaks through her Messiah who declares his love of truth and his will to destroy evil. Every enemy who stands against David's truth, embodied in the Son of David, is an enemy to the people of God.

I don't pray seeking revenge, but truth and justice! I shall declare my Lord as Lord and Messiah. I don't pray for vengeance over my enemies. My prayer is not for my personal plans and performance. It is an expression of trust in God whom I choose to be my representative and judge (v. 11). O Lord! Honour the blood of Christ by raising high the flag of righteousness and justice! Today I pray that you bless my enemies and empower me to show mercy to those who hate me. Enable me not only to be kind and loving but also to challenge evil, lifting high the name of Jesus and his righteousness.

～ Prayer from Psalm 59 ～

O God! Save me from my enemies (v. 1) and deliver me from evildoers! Save me from the men of blood (v. 2). Protect me from Cain, my brother, and from Esau, the son of my mother. The children of Jacob want to spill my blood, just like they wanted to do with Joseph. They act like Pharaoh and make my life full of hardship.

There are bloodthirsty men in my country. The tribe of the high priests has turned me into a Stephen, and I seek the Lord, crying out to him. The first Saul hit me and the second Saul threatens my children. Deliver me, O God! Blind his eyes with heavenly light so that he can see truth! Ask him, "Why do you persecute me?"

Herod killed James and put Peter in prison. He wanted to destroy my church and my dreams. But the angel of the Lord knocked him out and transformed my days.

The mighty gather against me not because of any iniquity or sin I have committed (v. 3) but because they reject my God. I shall not fight the sword with a sword, evil with evil, or a threat with a threat, because God himself will deal with my enemies (v. 10). He will destroy their evil with my faith, their pride with my humility. O Lord, bring an end to evil, lying, murder, and theft in my country! Remove the threat of the evil that howls like dogs hungry for blood during my dark nights (vv. 6, 14).

I shall not depend on my bow and sword but on my God. O God, I will praise your strength and mercy (v. 16). O God my strength! I sing unto you, for you are my refuge. You are the God who has shown me mercy; in my distress you are my salvation (vv. 16–17). Deliver your Middle Eastern church from its enemies. Send the angel of the Lord and change her destiny and my days. May the God of glory be revealed and may he transform every Saul of Tarsus.

I am like Ananias in the midst of your people. I am waiting for Saul to knock on my door. He shall not seek to kill me but to worship my God and my Lord. O God, deliver me from my enemies.

~ Prayer from Psalm 60 ~

O Lord! Who will bring me to the fortified city (v. 9)? Who will guide me to the unconquered rock of Edom? Our spiritual failures and misbehaviour pile up like skyscrapers. Rivers of blood fill our neighbourhoods and streets. We have lost the Middle East because extremism has spread and humanity has been distorted. Peace is lost; Satan has fortified himself with hatred, and the light of the gospel is growing dim.

Is there a David in our neighbourhoods or a Gideon in our churches? Where are our heroines? Where are Mary and Sarah? Satan's fortress is growing stronger as his evil worship centres spread. He has entered our holy places and filled them with grief and bitterness. We now seek ignorance instead of knowledge, division instead of unity, and we are no longer able or equipped to walk the path of love.

O Lord, why have you brought an earthquake to destroy the holiness of our country? Why have you broken the hearts of your beloved (vv. 2–3)? Why are your people and your followers so small in number and such a tiny minority? Why is Satan waging a continuous war against them with such perseverance? We have lost everything, even though we own everything!

Come, O Lord, and reveal your blessing. Restore the flag of your blessing over Nazareth and every city. Turn Mecca into a lighthouse for the gospel! I am a soldier in God's good news army. O Lord, come out and wage your war. Conquer the fortified city. Terminate evil, O mighty one! Empower us to plant churches void of despair.

The question is not the location of the fortified city, but who shall bring me to it? O Lord! Walk and I shall walk behind you, for the salvation of humans is in vain (v. 11). But the salvation of God is sure. You spoke your promises (v. 6), and you will keep them, as well as your threats. I shall conquer the fortified city, and the gates of hell shall not prevail. Today, I begin destroying the demonic gates, with my thoughts, words, and deeds, all in the name of Jesus.

~ Prayer from Psalm 61 ~

O Lord, I call upon you from the ends of the earth (v. 2)! From the land of alienation, I cry out to you. O ends of the earth! We are not helpless – we shall stand on a rock in the midst of your territory. God is our Rock. He is a refuge better than castles. O Lord! You are my refuge, and I watch over my country from your tower. You are a strong tower against the strongest foes (v. 3).

I enter your tent as your guest. I drink your coffee. You protect me and honour all of your guests (v. 4). That legend of generosity, the Arab Hatim Al Tai, is one of the least of your disciples. I take refuge from the jaws of Satan under your wings. I have come to you as a guest because I have heard about your generosity. You grant inheritance to your guests and to those who fear your name (v. 5). You increase their days from the fountain of time that springs from you (v. 6). Therefore, I have made vows and am now knocking at your doors.

I know that you have honoured me greatly, for you have turned me into one of your beloved ones. You have sent a king whose span of years is endless (v. 6). His authority, mercy, and truth embody your justice. He shall sit in your presence forever (v. 7). He is the expert in conflict resolution. He is your answer to the problems of the world. When he wore the garment of death, Satan planted his teeth in him. Those same teeth were broken by the power of the cross. Then Satan's wolves feared the least among your sheep.

Therefore I sing forever to your great name (v. 8). You are the end of alienation for all of your beloved ones. Love, rest, and salvation are in your tents. Peace and justice are in your territory. All of your guests are satisfied because of your generosity. Please receive me today as your guest in your inner room. The ends of the earth are only one step away from your territory. In my prayer I take this step and enter into your presence as your guest.

~ Prayer from Psalm 62 ~

O Lord! You are my refuge in whom I am protected (v. 7). Many attack me. Saul turned on me. Fear overwhelms me. Despair has become my food and clothing every day. When you refused my offer to build your temple, I was disappointed. Also, my child died. My heart was broken indeed. And the pain grew worse as I watched my children fight each other.

But I take refuge in you. I am like the woman caught in adultery, facing violent death. You are my refuge when they sentence me to death. The storms around me are strong, and my ship is about to sink, but you are my lifeguard and captain.

Like blind Bartemaeus, I shout and cry out! I want to see the hand of God. I declare my faith in you. Like the widow of Nain, my tears are calling you. Won't you touch the coffin in which my country is laid? I am fighting nations that have hosted demons since the time of my ancient ancestors. Legions of demons confront me, and my beloved ones are in shackles. Nazareth refused Jesus and continues to refuse his servants to this day. Jerusalem, Samaria, Lod, Jaffa, Caesarea, and Tiberias witnessed a revival, but not Nazareth. I wait for you in Nazareth (vv. 1, 5). I wait for you to save me from humiliation and from the pathological absence of faith. I pour my heart out in your presence (v. 8) to declare my trust in you. You graciously show mercy and punish evil (v. 12). You destroy and then build. You bring down and then lift up. I wait for you because you silence the lies of humans (v. 9), the hypocritical conspiracies, the transgression of arrogance, and the waywardness of those who are loaded with evil.

You are my refuge, therefore, I am not shaken before my enemies. I am not shaken before my thoughts and fears. I won't be defeated by the abundance of mischief and futility. I will drink your word like water, because it is my elixir. Your word is like the crushed grain that feeds me. It is as delicious as ice-cream topped with chocolate, and it awaits me. I am waiting upon the Lord, who is my saviour. He is my rock, my salvation, and my refuge. Therefore, I shall not be shaken (vv. 1–2, 5–6).

Prayer from Psalm 63

O Lord! I thirst for you (v. 1). I miss the touch of your Spirit. Your love dwells intimately in my heart. My eyes long to see your strength (v. 2). My ears yearn to hear your words. Please, speak to me! My body passionately desires to meet you. Come and embrace me. Have mercy on my thirst and give me a drink from the presence of your Spirit.

The mere thought of you, warms my spirit like a warm garment on a cold winter day. I ponder our time together and the intensity of my longing and love for you increases. Thinking of you is like clouds that drop rain full of love; my longing is like a torrential downpour that reminds me that you are my only satisfaction. You are my God (v. 1) and helper (v. 7). Without you, the fire of my joy and the light of my eyes will go out. Without you, my soul will dry up.

I tried to satisfy my hunger by consuming the food that people provide, but the glory of people and the world is futile. It does not satisfy my thirsty soul. Nothing that I have attained succeeds in replacing you, for you are the life of my soul.

When I give away my water to the injured who beg for help, my wound heals. Then my spirit blooms like a parched land on which merciful raindrops fall. I bless you, and I shall remember your mercy throughout my life (vv. 3–4). I shall raise my hands, and my lips shall sing songs of worship. I shall taste the food of heaven and drink from God's cup. My cup will be full.

In my thirst, I bless you, because my thirst is quenched. I praise you, and my mouth becomes full of blessing and the richest feast (v. 5). I shall remember you, so my strength increases. Without you I shall die, but with your blessing I shall drink and live.

～ Prayer from Psalm 64 ～

O Lord! How many are the conspiracies of evildoers (v. 2) and the enemies of the righteous! Cain killed his righteous brother. Joseph's brothers said, "Let's kill him and dump his body in one of the wells." Miriam and Aaron defied Moses, whom God himself addressed in person, not in riddles or mysteries! Korah and other evildoers honed their tongues like swords and filled their thoughts with wickedness (v. 3), grudges, and bitterness. They set snares (v. 5) for the righteous and trapped them with false words. They brought forward a woman who had been caught in adultery. Then they asked about paying tribute as well as taxes to Caesar, not knowing that the Lord would reveal the secrets of their hearts. They are better than Thomas Edison and Einstein in their ability to invent! But they create evil and blind those who see. O Lord!

My life shall be an ongoing prayer, trusting in my mighty God. If all the catastrophes of heaven, the temptations of hell, the crosses of earth, and the hardships of both this and the coming world, covered the heavens like a flock of birds, my heart would not fear! The arrow of God (v. 7) is like a tornado of fire. It is like a laser beam. Your light is stronger than evil's darkness; your light explodes and annihilates the darkness. It nullifies conspiracies, destroying them just as an earthquake splits the earth and destroys what humans have built. The power of conspiracies will be broken by our God who is able to split even the Red Sea.

God has dispatched only one arrow against evil. It became a guest in Nazareth and Bethlehem. It hung on a cross in Jerusalem. The good news spread, for this arrow cannot be turned aside! It does not fail; it turns the tide of battle and grants victory to God's people. My Christ is the arrow of God. May my life be the bowstring for this arrow. May the righteous God be declared in my every breath!

Prayer from Psalm 65

O Lord, forgive us our sins! Our iniquities have conquered us, but you forgive our transgressions (v. 3). Help us to be faithful to our vows and promises. Help us to offer our praises (v. 1) to you alone. May all human beings pray together with us in Zion! You who answers prayer (v. 2), hear our pleas.

Our country cannot rise from misery without your presence and blessings. Without your touch, our guilt will dominate our feelings and hurt our spirits. But in your house, we all become priests, and you satisfy us. You bring us closer to your heart (v. 4), for you are the God of our salvation, in whom we trust (v. 5). You address all our fears.

May blessings pour down on our country because you are in our midst! Come among us, dwell with us, and make your blessings a daily gift. Answer our prayers. Save our country and its people.

Without the water of heaven, our wounds will not heal. May the water of God fill our streams and moisten our pastures (vv. 10–12)! May the presence of God be the subject of our songs! Then our country will be healed, and our joy will multiply (vv. 12–13).

Your presence is the only guarantee; it is as indispensable as water and food. It is our strength and peace. It is the best fruit and the most important blessing. Water our spirit, and then we will flourish, producing love and righteousness. Then our churches will be full of those who are saved. Our country will be covered with love and peace. O Lord, my day is like a desert without you, but it is paradise when you are present!

~ Prayer from Psalm 66 ~

O people of God! Allow me to share with you what God has done in my life (v. 16). Come let me tell you how he has answered my prayers (vv. 19–20).

I have lived like Jonah in the belly of the fish, where I lost my strength and all my potential. I entered the belly of torture, and torture entered my belly. Distress was my food and drink. My loins were stressed, and people put burdens on my head (vv. 11–12). Who can rescue me? Who can relieve my despair?

O Lord! You alone can lift my head up. Hear me, for I present my vows to you (vv. 13–14). Without words, my tongue cries in pain. My God, my God, listen to my supplication.

The Lord spoke in my silence and affirmed the importance of getting rid of my iniquity. He will not listen to me if I cherish one sin in my heart (v. 18). I approached the throne of my God with my prayers. I offered my burnt offering before him (vv. 13–15). My offering is Jesus, who is fragrant with blessing. This offering is the answer to the cries of my heart.

God forgave my sins and healed the weakness of my faith. God offered a sacrifice to heal my soul. Then he acted by his Spirit. My soul trembled with gratitude. Today I stand in the circle of faith. I declare my faith in his temple and presence. I proclaim that he listens to our prayers. The Lord listens to everyone who repents. He listens to everyone who begs for mercy with tears, and in the name of Jesus.

Hallelujah! God listened, and he heard my prayer (v. 19). Blessed is God whose mercy never ends, and whose grace never expires.

Now is my time. It is the time of blessing; it is the season of salvation, for the Lord listens to my prayer. He will not distance his mercy from me (v. 20).

~ Prayer from Psalm 67 ~

May God have mercy on us and bless us! May he spread the light of his countenance upon us (v. 1)!

O Lord! Bless us (vv. 1, 6, 7). Bless us with your presence. Declare your compassion, and let your grace be among us. Let all the people know that our salvation is in Jesus. He is the way to salvation (v. 2).

O God! Bless us so that we may bless others. Then your blessing will be cloned and will multiply so that all nations will praise the Lord (v. 3).

No one can monopolize the joy of the Lord; all nations will rejoice in the Lord. Laughter will dwell with us. The pleasure of heaven and earth will be our companion. Bless us, so that we may lead the nations to you, so that we may see the dominion of justice in our land (v. 4). Let the nations praise you, O God! This is our request (v. 5). Bless us with a covenant in which you are our Lord and God (v. 6).

Bless us like our mothers, Eve, Sarah, Rebekah, Jochebed, Hannah, Elizabeth, and Mary, the mother of our Lord. Then we will give birth to blessing and build up our people with the grace of God. Bless us like Solomon, Abraham, Isaac, David, and Joseph. Grant us success. Bless us like Peter and Paul, so that we may love God wholeheartedly.

Have mercy on us today, and bless us. Multiply our blessing like you did the five loaves and two fish. You have blessed every poor and sinful person. Bless us! Be sovereign over us, and be our King today.

⤝ Prayer from Psalm 68 ⤜

O Lord! Gladden me, and make me jump with joy (v. 3), for you are the father of orphans, the vindicator of widows, and the one who frees prisoners (vv. 5–6). Grant me victory, and disperse the darkness of evil. May your face shine and be my sun (v. 1)!

Your presence is the greatest victory. It is like a fountain of goodness to the poor (v. 10). The wilderness of my life is transformed by your generosity, which showers blessing because of your grace (v. 9).

I don't need to fight for your blessing because you have already fought in my place. You have dispersed many kings (v. 14). For my sake, you fought against hell and earth. You ascended on high and took many captive (v. 18). The gates of hell shook in fear! Blessed is the Lord, both day and night (v. 19). He created a way of escape from death (v. 20). He crushed the enemies, rebuked the beasts of evil, and protected his people (v. 30).

Won't you clap your hands for the Lord? Won't you honour God (v. 34)? Why don't we testify in gratitude that God has given us a word (v. 11)? Then the Word clothed itself with a human body. It became human, and we saw God's glory.

He gave some to be apostles who declared the love of God. They encouraged us not to remain children in righteousness or inexperienced infants in praise. Hallelujah! O Lord, open my heart! Then I shall receive your grace.

Today you gladden me and give me strength and determination (v. 35). I lay down my agenda and the dreams of my day; you are my number one priority. I fully rejoice in you!

~ Prayer from Psalm 69 ~

A flood of distress overwhelms me (v. 1). My throat is dry from much praying (v. 3). I am still waiting for my God (v. 3). My day is no longer sunny, for the sun has disappeared from my life. I live in darkness. But I lift my eyes up to the stars, waiting for my God.

I know that his promises will not fail, and that even in the midst of my pain, my hope grows. I know that the light of his stars will not appear to me except in darkness. I know that those who wait upon the Lord will not be ashamed (v. 6).

I have also learned that one prayer is better than dozens of quick decisions. In prayer, I discover my weakness, death, and impotence. In the midst of prayer, my God appears. He strengthens me, and in the midst of the destructive torrent, he delivers my life (v. 14).

O God abundant in mercy, I pray to you (vv. 13, 16)! I fast with tears (v. 10), and you recognize my disgrace (v. 19). They put gall in my food and gave me vinegar for my thirst (v. 21). O God, let your salvation come! Lift me up from this painful reality. Save my country and show abundant mercy. Let the festivities of the wicked end and the joyful celebration of heaven begin with the repentance of one sinner! Then may my whole country follow! May death die, and the power of sin be destroyed! May you answer my prayers and turn the church into a living church! Then those who seek God will be empowered, and the meek will share my joy (v. 32).

I know that the Lord does not despise our prayers; he listens and delivers us! God shall deliver Zion, end destruction, and build a new future (v. 35). O Lord, bless my country! On this day I lift up my eyes to heaven.

⟿ Prayer from Psalm 70 ⟿

O Lord! Hurry up, come to me, and don't linger (vv. 1, 5). My strength is evaporating. Those who seek to hurt me are using words that strike deep into my bones. Evildoers mock my trust in you and the way I embrace you. They despise and insult me. Their words are like knives (v. 3). "Marana-tha" (come O Lord) and don't delay. The Spirit and the bride seek your presence.

I know that you are sailing towards me. By faith, I see your ship's sail speeding closer. It cuts its way through the swells of the sea. But when will you reach the island where I wait? When will you fix my heartbreak? Come and save me, for I can no longer control my longing for you.

O Great One, be glorified and let your name be exalted (v. 4)! Open the door of my ark and consider the flood around me. Open the grave, and call Lazarus to come out and jump with joy. I am like Peter, Herod's prisoner. Won't you open the doors of my prison and cover me with your miraculous grace?

Let my country also be filled with the miracles of heaven. Let your people hear about your glory and proclaim it. Open all the channels of blessing. Let my weakness shrink into insignificance. I am poor, but by your grace I am enriched. Because of your presence, my life will not be impoverished (v. 5).

"Marana-tha!" O Lord, come to my day and help my love for you grow. Please turn "Marana-tha" (come O Lord) to Maran-atha (the Lord came)? I am waiting while I contemplate the cross of my Jesus.

~ Prayer from Psalm 71 ~

O Lord, I am a refugee fleeing to you! I trust and take refuge in you (v. 1). You are my rock and refuge; I come to you (v. 3). You are my fortress that will not collapse, despite the showers of missiles.

When wicked people look at me, I can almost feel their hands strangling me; but evil hands cannot reach you (v. 4). Red and gory, Cain is pursuing me, but you are my hope in whom I trust (v. 5). I take refuge in you daily; you have never failed in shepherding me. Since my birth, they have conspired against you and me, but they have continually failed because of you (vv. 5–10). Don't reject me or forsake me, for I need you (v. 9). Don't distance yourself from me, for my heart longs for you (v. 12).

Grey has invaded my hair. It is the outcome of the work of your hands. Every hair tells the story of your touch, which is full of righteousness as well as kindness (vv. 17–19). You have shown us many painful hardships. Yet you return and restore our lives, granting us your generous gifts (v. 20).

From the depth of Sheol, you raise us up, placing us inside the pupil of your eye. You exalt and comfort us; despair cannot rule over us as long as our hearts are in your hands (v. 21). I praise you and sing to you with a lute. I exult in your righteousness, for I am in your hands today (vv. 22–24).

~ Prayer from Psalm 72 ~

O Lord! Grant us a leader who has not only sight but also insight. Give us a leader who distinguishes between what is and is not significant. We want a leader who loves virtue and avoids vice. Bless us with someone who builds up, heals, loves you, and follows you. We long for someone who will rule your people with justice and build your house with truth (v. 2).

He will confront the oppressor and save your children (v. 4). In his days, the mountains will be filled with peace (v. 3). The sun and the moon will fear you (v. 5). The thirst of your land (v. 6) will be quenched with rain, and the ends of the earth shall praise your king (vv. 9–11). He represents the voice of the poor and the ones who seek your help (v. 12). He shows mercy to the wretched and provides for their needs (v. 13). He is a gift who honours your men and women (v. 14).

O God! Let us rejoice with our leader and bless you (v. 15). Let our earth flourish, our trees bring forth fruit, and let us receive your blessings.

Jesus, our leader, filled our earth with your glory (v. 19). He died, rose from the dead, and ascended into heaven. Then your Spirit came upon us.

Give us a leader who follows Jesus and who fills the earth with your glory. Won't you produce such leaders in the name of your Messiah? Send us a hero, a leader who is filled with the Spirit, and a person who obeys and submits to your Son. Give us a leader after your own heart. Then he shall heal your vine and spread your peace throughout our country. Let your name alone be lifted up in our country.

Today, we pray for our leaders: the shepherds of our churches, the leaders of our countries, and the leaders of your people. Also, turn me into a leader after your own heart, for you alone are the worker of miracles (v. 18). Amen and Amen.

~ Prayer from Psalm 73 ~

O Lord! If you are good, then why don't you remove oppression (v. 1)? If you are powerful, why do you allow iniquity?

The righteous are afflicted, while the wicked are at peace (v. 3). We endure toil and hardship, but the arrogant relax and their bodies are full of fat (vv. 4–5). We are clothed with humility, but they put on oppression and iniquity (v. 6). We become thin as we fast and are hungry, while they fill their cheeks and even their eyelids with fat (v. 7). They attack heaven and earth with the thoughts of their hearts and the words of their mouths (vv. 7–12). Are we following you in vain, for our lives are full of worry and pain (vv. 13–14)?

But your goodness is not an abstract philosophy; it's a tangible reality that appeared through the shedding of blood. Partial knowledge is a misleading poison, but mature discernment advocates faith and fights gossip. I have entered the holies of the Most High and have been enlightened. My worries have disappeared (v. 17). I have seen the light of God.

Now I understand that the oppression of the wicked lasts only for a moment. Their establishment is only an illusion (vv. 17–20). When I consider the experience of Moses, Isaiah, and Asaph, I recognize that you are indeed the Holy Father who is full of goodness. You are the fountain of mercy and the mother who gave birth to compassion. You are beauty itself, so why am I focusing my eyes on the ugliness of oppression? You are eternal satisfaction, so why am I lusting for a dish that will only satisfy my soul's hunger for a moment or maybe a day? You are Love that bleeds in order to save all humans. You are my portion; therefore I shall not seek someone else for the rest of my days (vv. 25–26).

From birth to burial, you are good to all of your creatures. Even when I was still in the womb and after burial, when I will live forever and ever, you will always be good to me. I will seek your face today and every day.

～ Prayer from Psalm 74 ～

O Lord! They set your holy temple on fire and defiled your name (v. 7). They burned, exploited, and tore down what you have made.

How long will the enemy insult your name (v. 10)? How long will evil people underestimate Jesus? You split the sea with your power (v. 13). You created a gushing fountain in the midst of the wilderness. By your grace, you unleashed a torrent of water (v. 15). You turned Pharaoh and his gods into a worm under our feet. You revealed your dominion over day and night, and over the sun as well as the moon (v. 16). Your dominion spans summer and winter. All the earth belongs to you (v. 17).

I am but a worm. Can a worm fight a dragon? Can it conquer the dragon without your help?

The enemy insults us; an ignorant nation despises your name (v. 18). Will you abandon your beloved dove in the lion's jaws (v. 19)? Will you allow the devil to devour your chicks? You are the Holy Spirit, and we are your young children. We are crushed and impoverished for the sake of your name (v. 20).

Arise, O God! Rise up, O mighty one! Let your name be lifted up (v. 22). Stand up and replace evil with good. Rise up and destroy even the idea of murder, using your cross, the fountain of love that flows from your church. Rise up in my life, my church, and my country. Destroy hatred – but don't forget your wretched flock (v. 19). O Lord, arise, present your case, and remember the insults of the ignorant (v. 22). Rise up, and don't forget the rage of your adversaries (v. 23). Rise, O God; this is your war. Please, arise today!

May your face be always before us! Rise up to protect your people and to bless your enemies with goodness and eternal light.

～ Prayer from Psalm 75 ～

O Lord, you are the judge (v. 7). Many necks are stiff. Many minds are like stone. But you are the highest authority, past, present, and future. You humble whoever you want and lift up he who pleases you (v. 7).

Your hand is the weighing balance for the pillars of the earth, as well as for the smallest thoughts (v. 3). You establish a court with integrity as the foundation of its judicial system (v. 2). You confront the arrogant and the evil, calling them to humility (v. 4). You ignore the evil of neither the East nor the West. You don't overlook sin in the mountains or the valleys (v. 6). Indeed, you bring all oppressors to account and vindicate every oppressed person.

Thus we cry out and call upon you. I praise you, and my heart sings as I contemplate your wonders (v. 1). I trust your justice even if oppressors dwell in my country. I trust that you have an appointed season (v. 2) to declare the rage of heaven and to confirm that you will take care of the poor, the widowed, and the orphaned.

You do care! Your judgment does not focus on the amount of evil or how long it lasts but on the damage it does to your name and your people. It takes only a moment to kill a human being, but the punishment is life imprisonment. The amount of damage is the foundation for a just judgment. We have forgotten that we spat in the face of the redeemer. We despised the blood of the crucified creator. We murdered the beloved Son.

You, O God, are the judge. Hell is our portion, but still you care! You are not a merciless judge; pardon is granted for those who honour the redeemer and saviour. Either we encounter the judge with the help of the redeemer, or we encounter the coming wrath. Whoever has the Son has life, and whoever does not have the Son will encounter the wrath of the judge (v. 8).

~ Prayer from Psalm 76 ~

O Lord! Even human wrath brings you praise (v. 10). The hard hearts of people are opportunities for your grace. I understand that obedience praises you, but how can the hardness of hearts exalt you?

Pharaoh's foolishness and stubbornness were the path for demonstrating your strength. Sennacherib thought that he could attack you with his army. How many kings have wanted to extinguish the light of your church? The enemies of truth, righteousness, love, and justice become channels for your miracles and love. Through their transgressions you reveal your justice and commitment to your church. The stronger they become, the clearer your demonstration of divine power. Whenever their evil increases, your grace overflows. Whenever their resistance escalates, you move the tip of your divine finger. The season of tribulation is the season in which I behold your miracles and strength.

Won't you end all wars with your love (v. 3)? Won't you reveal justice and make people respect heaven through your anger (v. 7)? Humankind became angry and murdered your Messiah. They broke his body as if it were a clay pot, and then the perfume of praise spread out. They put out the lamp of his life, but through his death, the sun of righteousness and a new creation dawned.

You are awesome! Who can stand before you (v. 7)? The seas of darkness are split by your ship of light. The waves of war are silenced by your rebuke (v. 6). You are awesome, and we are waiting for you to rise. You will rise to deliver the meek of the earth and to spread your peace (v. 9). O Lord, wage your war against wars. End killing and make hatred abhorred. This is the path of divine wrath. Your wrath and grace are companions that cannot be separated. Your grace is angered by evil, and salvation is the fruit of your anger. It is not only the fruit of love, but also of anger against sin.

O Lord! I have heard the symphony of anger on Friday; now I am waiting for its song on Sunday when I praise you. I will look at my Friday while I stand on the rock of praise on Sunday. I will praise you.

~ Prayer from Psalm 77 ~

O Lord! Have you locked your mercies in a cage (v. 8)? Did you wrap your compassion with forgetfulness (v. 9)? Has your rejection of your people become like a volcanic mountain? Has your mercy become as small as a speck of sand? Is there not one single umbrella of mercy that provides shelter at the noon of your rage?

Just a moment of your rejection is like an eternity of pain. The streets of hell become my path in your anger. Will you reject your people forever (v. 7)? Has the date of your mercy expired (v. 8)?

I am a Canaanite woman who has a daughter possessed by demons (Mark 7:26). I seek your mercy. I am a blind Bartimaeus begging for your compassion (Mark 10:47). You showed mercy to your servant Lot (Gen 19:16) and to Epaphroditus when you healed him (Phil 2:27). We too are your people! Nurse us with your compassion and embrace us. Don't call us Lo-Ruhamah (Hos 1:6); instead, fill our lives with divine mercy.

I shall recall your works and wonders, and I shall remember you (vv. 3, 6, 11). Will you forget us while we remember you? We contemplate your works (v. 12) and hunger for your mercy. Your compassion is better than life.

O Lord, Pharaoh is wandering in your land! The devil holds the necks of your daughters. Loudspeakers are everywhere, rejecting your religion. The body of Christ is blistered with divisions, and your people are busy amputating your body. Where are the winds of heaven and the thunder of your voice (v. 18)? Where is the arm of God (v. 15)? Where are your wonders, acts of power, and fountains of mercy (v. 14)?

I cannot be convinced that you have forgotten your mercies, and so I wait for you. Have mercy on me and on my country. Have mercy on us and guide your people (v. 20). Bring millions of believers to your church. O Lord – *Kyrie eleison* (Κύριε ἐλέησον). Have mercy, O Lord!

~ Prayer from Psalm 78 ~

O Lord! Our fathers and mothers proclaimed you (v. 3). Arabs have known you for thousands of years. They have praised you (v. 4). Job, the Queen of Sheba, Lemuel and his mother, they all told us about you. Let the next generation know and rise up to tell their children about you (v. 6). Let them depend upon the Lord and not forget the works of God. Let them keep his commandments (v. 7) even in the face of death.

Defending the rights of the wife of Antipas, the Baptist was killed. He died to protect the Arab daughter of Aretas and to defend her. Moses, the one known as the bishop of the Arabs, challenged the whole world. Our hearts have been illuminated by a list of Arab heroes who wrote for us the pillars of faith. Abu Qurah and John of Damascus are two of many Arab theologians. Hundreds of Arab Christians have been martyred defending the orthodox faith.

But today we have gone astray and have acted against you. We have lost our history and way. We forgot the blood of our ancestors, whose necks were put under the sword because they were faithful to your covenant. Abed Al Massih, the martyr of Ramlah, and Rami, the martyr of Gaza, are singing together in heaven, but we forgot their path and rebelled. Our lives and paths are pure madness! Instead of walking in the footsteps of our ancestors, we chose the cursed path. We picked another religion, and our wicked are experts in religiosity.

But you, O God, are compassionate and merciful. You forgive our iniquities and continue to offer us your help (v. 38). Have mercy on Arabs and build their churches to give them joy again. Distance them from evil and help them remove themselves from iniquity. Send your Messiah to their land and bless them, for we are waiting.

⌐ Prayer from Psalm 79 ⌐

O Lord! Evildoers defile your house and despise your name (v. 1). They murder your sons and subjugate your daughters (v. 2). We are small in number and limited in intellectual abilities, and we fall short in virtue. But we are a majority in the number of our dead. We have the greatest pain and fears. Stop pouring your wrath out against us. We have become despised, disgraced, and a cause for laughter. How long will your anger burn and your wrath be like fire that burns us (vv. 3–5)? We have been turned from a church of flesh into empty church buildings and museums. Many visit us as if they are visiting museums of an ancient and extinct civilization. The sharp tusks of evildoers are tearing us apart. Divisions multiply like worms. Wolves and foxes destroy your land (v. 7).

O God, we repent and return to you! Help us, for you are the God of our salvation. We bow down at your feet (v. 9). Deliver us and forgive our sins for the sake of your name (v. 9). Why should evildoers deride us? They ask, "Where is your God?" (v. 10). We have become the children of death instead of being your household.

Are we not your people and the sheep of your flock (v. 12)? Don't we carry your name? We have accepted your discipline for hundreds of years, but where is your help? We have returned to you with tears, but where is your revival? Our blood is poured out like rivers, but where is your water of life? Have mercy and bring forth revival. Our biggest loss is your absence. Our greatest pain is missing your kind touch. But far be it from you to reject your anointed ones and forget your sons and daughters. Forgive us and have mercy on your people. Have mercy on your home country. Honour your name by changing your evildoers. We continue to praise you and speak about your praises (v. 13).

⁓ Prayer from Psalm 80 ⁓

O shepherd of Israel, listen to your sheep (v. 1). We have eaten the bread of tears; we have drunk our tears in big mugs (v. 5). You have poured your wrath upon us, and we have been in the midst of woe (v. 4). How long will we encounter troubles, both day and night?

We have become like a vine without a fence, and our land is without a river or even a stream (v. 12). The beasts of evil have devoured our strength; we no longer have any power (v. 13). Restore us to you and save us, for you are the light of every season and every generation (vv. 3, 7, 14, 19).

We were the head of all the nations. Our success was like the sharply rising line of a graph. But we lost our way; we sinned against you. Instead of being the head, we have become the tail. My people and I are sheep who have lost their path. We have no strength for riding horses or for war. Without you, our stomachs are full of pain. Our goodness is as dark as midnight.

Send us your right-hand man, the chosen one, who can destroy all woe (vv. 17–18). He alone can give us your blessing, along with many crowns. He will destroy all evil both around us and in us. He is the sword of God that is ready for battle. He is our oasis and our place of shade. He heals the souls of all who are weak. He is our only hope of divine success, and he is the healer of everyone who is troubled. Send him to us so that he can heal our sickness and quiet our wailing. Send him to restore the light that is reflected on us from your face and to reinstate every beautiful thing. We want to see Jesus exalted and honoured. O Shepherd of your people, will you listen to your sheep?

⁓ Prayer from Psalm 81 ⁓

S ing unto God, the source of our strength! Shout to the Lord, the fountain of our pride (v. 1)! Let the tambourine dance to our melodies; let the strings jump to the sound of our praises (v. 2). How great art thou, O God! Every day, you are our holiday. We have called upon you, and you have removed our burdens.

We lost our way, but you swiftly guided us. You delivered our fathers from the bondage of Pharaoh. In our distress, you have delivered us. Today, you warn us (v. 8), so we declare to all people, "Don't worship any other gods; worship the Lord alone. Don't seek what makes him angry!" Our hearts did not listen and were turned to stone; our ears were filled with rocks (v. 11). We became accustomed to having hard hearts. Even our dreams depicted visions of a future full of hardness. These dreams became our nightmares, and these nightmares have become our daily reality. Indeed, our distress has mounted, and in the furnace of hardship our praise has evaporated.

Ah, if our people would only listen to your words (v. 13)! If our children would only honour your name, if we would for your sake give up our pride, if we would return to you and bow down, if we would lift up the name of Jesus, if we would listen to your commandments and love you, if we would humble ourselves and become one body, if we would cry out seeking your blessing, if we would pray with tears – then you would re-establish our singing. With your Spirit, you would rekindle our praises. The joy of our hearts and the cry of our victories would return (v. 14), along with copious blessings (v. 16).

Ah, if we would return to you, then our meetings would be filled with people, our baskets would be overflowing with offerings, our churches would be filled with blessings, and we would discover that you are the greatest God.

Please restore us and awaken our souls from their deep sleep. For the sake of Jesus, restore us to your bosom. Even if the heart becomes a solid rock, God will not fail. O Lord, today you are our holiday.

~ Prayer from Psalm 82 ~

O Lord! You want justice and want us to walk in its footsteps (v. 2). You care for the orphan, the poor, and the widowed (v. 3). Empower me to become an eye for the blind and a tear for those who sit in darkness. Turn me into legs for the crippled and for those who suffer immobility. Enable me to be a mother for the poor and for orphans. Give me the strength to be a voice for the mute and for those whose tongues have been silenced. I desire to be a home for a homeless nation. I want to be a comforting smile during a season of sadness, a moment of rest in an eternity of torture. May I become a garment of mercy for the helpless.

My world has become an island of the rich surrounded by a sea of the poor. Half the people on earth live below the poverty line; many are living on less than a dollar a day. They lack water, homes, and education. Without the eye of justice, we don't see their plight; without the ear of mercy, we don't hear their voice. Should we enjoy our island of richness and ignore the waves crashing on our beach, waves full of pain, weakness, and poverty? Our neighbours are sinking in a sea of sorrows. They want justice and search for it.

"Who is my neighbour?" the church continues to ask. But I plead for justice and seek to walk in it. O God, rise up and transform your church to become a seeker of justice who walks in its path (v. 8). Help me today to wake up from the drunken seeking of riches so that I can start showing mercy to the weak, the orphan, the widow, the handicapped, the refugee, and the unemployed. Help me to seek justice for poor nations, for their sons and daughters.

⌐ Prayer from Psalm 83 ⌐

O Lord! Hellish forces attack your people (v. 2). They seek to wipe out those you love (v. 4). Ten nations conspire against your people (vv. 5–8). They wage war against the people of God; they hate the God of my people (v. 2).

The army of Jabin rides in 900 iron chariots (v. 9; Judg 4:3). But Deborah has a word from the Lord, and our people go up to her. She will win and the enemies will lose. The wedge of Jael will kill Sisera, and he will die. Hellish people lost the battle in the valley of Kishon, but they did not give up their evil. They attacked again like Orev and Zeev; Orev the raven and Zeev the wolf attacked the people of God.

All hell joins the battle against the anointed one of God. They cover his cross like flies to celebrate. They trample over the blood of the Messiah, thinking they have won. But they are ignorant of God's power. The King of glory shall rise, and they will blow away like chaff in the wind (v. 13). By his resurrection, he has lit the fire of life, and the wicked shall burn to death. They fight God and will lose. They will be filled with fear and shame, for the Lord alone is the King of kings.

But they don't know this (v. 18). My prayers are not motivated by vengeance; I long for evildoers to seek your salvation (v. 16). My prayer is that your people win for the sake of the name of Jesus. May your name last forever, and may your enemies be ashamed.

~ Prayer from Psalm 84 ~

O Lord, I want three blessings (vv. 4, 5, 12).

First, I want to build a nest in your dwelling place (v. 3). Like a sparrow or swallow, I want my young to be next to your altar (v. 3). I want to be a priest in your temple, for my soul longs for your dwelling place (v. 2). It is a place of life, freedom, and grace. Your protection is the best of all shelters. The best and purest life is when my heart and flesh are busy praising you (v. 6). In the face of death, I declare that you alone are the living God.

Second, I want to proclaim you as my strength and honour. May your house dwell in my heart (v. 5). May the power of God fill me, for the journey is difficult! But with your support, it is also a great adventure (v. 7)! You transform problems into blessings. Every worshipper is a drop of life that overflows because of your life. Like copious rain, we drown every kind of death, and we walk on towards you.

Third, I want your protection and the honour of depending upon you. I choose one day in your dwelling place over one thousand away from you! I choose the crumbs of your table, which are better than the fatted calves of your foes. Their feasts are poisonous, but life is in your crumbs. You are my honour, and I find shelter in you. You are the fountain of goodness and mercy, and I shall quench my thirst in you. Blessed is everyone who depends on you (v. 12). I shall be your guest every day.

On this day, I want three blessings (vv. 4, 5, 12): to live in your house, to be strengthened by you, and to depend upon you.

~ Prayer from Psalm 85 ~

O Lord, you showed favour to your land and forgave the iniquities of your people (vv. 1–2). You set your wrath aside and covered all the sins of your people (vv. 1–3). You removed the punishment and put a dam before the rivers of your rage. Then we returned with Ezra, but we still lack your presence! Won't you return, that your people may rejoice in you (v. 6)?

You removed death from us, but without your presence we are still dead. The sunset of darkness does not mean the sunrise of your peace. Crucifying demons and locking up hellish people is one of your blessings, but it cannot replace the fragrance of your breath and Spirit. Our bones are dry, and our trees are miserable without you. You are our groom, so please come to your bride.

Will you return to us? Then we will be revived and taste your peace. Will you come back and live again in your Galilee? Will you illuminate our darkness with your light? Will you refresh our praises from your fountain and pour divine strength on our songs? Will the Shekinah dwell again in our land? Will your peace make its home in our church (v. 9)?

I dream of a day when mercy and truth meet again, a day when both righteousness and peace live among your people. I dream of a day when our churches are full of your goodness. On that day, sermons from your Word will be music to our ears. Your blessing will rewrite our story. Our faces will shimmer with your reflection, and our hearts will be energized by your dreams. The Father and the Son will be in our midst; we will be led by your Spirit. The poor and the miserable will discover that we are the house of God. The ends of the earth will hear your voice. The nations will recognize the Messiah in your children.

Will you return and revive us? Then your land will be filled with salvation. Heaven will rejoice as your life flows through us! Today, I pray for a spiritual awakening for all your people.

Prayer from Psalm 86

O Lord, save your servant who trusts in you (v. 2). Have mercy on me, for I call upon you (v. 3). You are the Lord of life, and I need you. I am drowning in the sea of misery, but a lifeline is in your hands. You will deliver me from the depths of Sheol and lift me up to you (v. 13). All the nations will bow down before you (v. 9). O Lord, open your eyes to us, and let all who call upon you bask in the light of your eyes (v. 5).

My prayers have wandered all through the market of other gods, but they always come back to you. There is none like you among the gods; no deeds can compare with the works of your hands (v. 8). Every relationship is like chaff in comparison to the gold of your forgiveness and the words of your lips. Every great person is like dust in comparison to you. You are the conqueror of time and the master of every place, for you alone are God (v. 10).

Teach me to love you and walk in your truth (v. 11). Train me to fear your name and seek your glory (v. 11). Nurse me with your praise's milk and let my tongue shout your glory (v. 12). You are compassionate and merciful; how great is your name (v. 15)! Grant me a sign of your goodness, and let your servant be exalted by your grace (v. 17).

You are the feeder of my soul. You alone are the healer of the wounded. You are the soul of true faith, the destroyer of illusions, and the maker of revivals. All nations, all tongues, all social classes, every elder, every adult, every young person, every infant, and whatever moves or does not move will bow down and glorify your name. Let your name be exalted today.

~ Prayer from Psalm 87 ~

O Lord, you are the one who opens wombs. Therefore Sarah, Rebekah, and Rachel had children and weaned their boys. Life dwelt in the wombs of Hannah, Elizabeth, and the wife of Mannoah. Their hard days were transformed into joy.

The body brings forth a child, but for God to bring forth a nation, this is like a dream! Every person who is born of the Spirit is a walking miracle, not an illusion.

O Lord, you have given birth to a whole nation in Zion. There you destroyed all forms of vengeance. You have given birth to the civilization of love and have turned foes into friends. Rahab, Babylon, Philistia, and the children of Israel acknowledge that you are the Lord of peace. There are no ethnic barriers or bigotry. Evil has run away. It has become a transient shadow in a dream. An inclusive civilization has been born, one that includes sisters as well as brothers. It has no place for evildoers. After a long season of war, murder, and hatred, a feast of love has been born. Jesus is the seed of the new creation, and through him, Zion is filled with songs and praises.

We don't want only the birth of souls, but also the birth and embodiment of the civilization of our dreams. The kingdom of God is righteousness, love, and all sorts of peace. O Lord, won't you make Zion a lighthouse in every corner of the world? Won't you imprison Satan and his fiery arrows? Let there be no more killing, or wars, or hatred, or bigotry. I will not stop dreaming! O Lord, bless your church! Let her move forward by your grace and strength.

~ Prayer from Psalm 88 ~

O Lord, Dante says that the words "Abandon hope, all ye who enter here" are written on the gates of hell. Hell is not just a place; it is also an existence that overflows with hardship. I am tired and ill (v. 3). I am counted among the dead, and my mattress lies between graves. I live in pain. My eyes melt away in disgrace (v. 9). Humiliation surrounds me like a garment. The wrath of God has become my daily food, and I have forgotten the taste of joy (v. 7). My faith is butchered by the edge of days, and my strength has been shattered. I am surrounded by destruction, catastrophe and hardship, and misery is an epidemic. There is blood, betrayal, and treachery, and the world has been emptied of any justice.

Ah! I cry out to you, for you have the keys of happiness (vv. 1, 13). You alone are able to conquer every hardship. You are able to save all who are sheltered in the Messiah, without exception. My cry rises out of the depths of catastrophe to the one whose hands hold heaven and earth, the one who is able to resolve all problems. I cry out from the land of the forgotten (v. 12), from Sheol (v. 3), from the lowest pit (v. 4), from the grave (v. 5), from the darkest depths (v. 6), and from a desolate land.

I pour out my tears and collect my prayers in a jar. I wish I had a rope that could lift my jar up to heaven. Or perhaps God could come down to my pit and drink my prayers like soup! Indeed, I shall continue to pray in the name of Jesus, for I know that the Lord of life will not accept the dominion of death. Won't you return and revive us? Won't you restore our joy and singing?

Prayer from Psalm 89

I shall sing of the mercies of the Lord (v. 1). The covenant of the Lord is my covenant (v. 3). The showers of blessings are mine and my children's (v. 4). He has anointed my forehead with his sacred oil (v. 20). His hand strengthens my hand. His arm empowers me (v. 21). I shall tell him that you are my Father, my salvation and my God (v. 26). You are my love, my eyes, and the pulse of my heart. You are the soul of my spirit, the inner life of my life, and the secret of my success. You are my shelter when I am weak. When I am powerless, you are my hiding place. I am your servant, and you are my Lord and God. You are the Lord of the cross, and Jesus is your beloved, as well as mine. He is the seal of the covenant between you and me.

But you have allowed boulders to crush my signet ring (v. 38). You have allowed the hand of my adversaries to be lifted up against me (v. 42). Disgrace dwells in my bosom (v. 50). My days are now clothed with shame (v. 45). How can I face my death without your covenant? Can anyone deliver themself from the destruction of death (v. 48)?

But where humans fail, God will not fail. The Lord of the resurrection will grant me life after death. The mercy of God and his covenant are greater than my death. His light is stronger than my darkness, and his love always heals.

Shine your merciful light on my life. Today I want to praise you and sing to you. I shall sing of the mercies of the Lord, and proclaim his truth with my mouth. You will always be my God, and I will always remain faithful to your covenant. Amen, and again, Amen!

~ Prayer from Psalm 90 ~

O Lord, our days may total seventy or eighty years if our strength endures (v. 10). We work hard and struggle, but we are walking towards death. Every mighty man and great woman is but dust, for all are but dust. Our lives are like grass that springs up for one day, then disappears. In addition, we are consumed by your anger and terrified of your indignation; your absence is our death (v. 7).

You are our only shelter when death attacks. You are the artist who paints time with an eternal paintbrush. One thousand years in your eyes are no different from millions of years (v. 4). Millions of years are like a fleeting second. If you are indignant for a moment, we are lost for eternity. We live for a mere 100 years as if we were immortal.

Teach us to count our days and recognize that God's wisdom is food for eternal life. Train us to live by the standards of heaven, for we are aware of our end. We are indeed mortal, but by your unending grace, we can touch eternity and drink immortality. In your bosom, we are heavenly immortals.

Thus we seek today seven things: Return O Lord, and we will return to you (v. 13a). Have compassion on your servants, and we will humble ourselves before you (v. 13b). Satisfy us with your mercy, for we are hungry and thirsty for righteousness (v. 14). Gladden us with your covenant and grace, for we are bent down with humility (v. 15). Reveal your strength, works, and glory, for you are our Father and we are your sons and daughters (v. 16). Pour your blessings on us. We are not worthy, but you are generous and always compassionate (v. 17). O Lord, establish the works of our hands. Because of your support, we will conquer death. In you alone we are immortal.

~ Prayer from Psalm 91 ~

He will save you from the fowler's snare (v. 3). He will protect you from pestilence; demons of the night and the midday cannot hurt you (v. 6). Pestilence and destruction cannot destroy you (v. 6). You will not fear, and worry will not consume you. Before failure and before every form of evil, God's immunity will be enough for you. Many will perish, but evil will not approach you (v. 7). You are under the protection of the Lord. He will guard you. With his wings, he will hide you (v. 4).

The mountain of difficulties and burdens is no longer on your shoulders but under your feet. O Lord, all the demons of the world are afraid of the authoritative words of your mouth. God shall command his angels concerning you (v. 11). Success and victory belong to you. Divine sonship, heavenly gifts, and even his forgiveness will be given to you. You will tread on the world's glory. The head of the snake shall be under your feet because of the works of the Lord's hand.

Therefore, today I shall cling to your arm (v. 14). I know that you will rescue, exalt, respond to, deliver, glorify, satisfy, and save the one who clings to even a finger of your hand (vv. 14–16). Your protection is greater than that offered by the best lawyers, the smartest physicians, or the lowest mercenaries. Your guarantee is better than all treasures, the best health, or even family. You never betray your people or give up on them. Your protection does not end. There is nothing that distracts or deters you from your faithfulness.

This day I put into your hands every fear, worry, anxiety, and burden, for my rest is found in you. I will not let the worry of tomorrow kill the joy of today. Be the shield of your sons and daughters. You are my shelter, my refuge, and my God in whom I trust (v. 2).

～ Prayer from Psalm 92 ～

I praise you every day, and I do not murmur or complain. I exalt your mercy in the morning and magnify your faithfulness before sleeping (v. 2). I exult and rejoice in the Lord (vv. 3–4). You have made me glad by the works of your hands. The time of fasting is now over, and the blessings of the Lord are piling up like a mountain of joy. How deep are your thoughts, O Lord! They are like an ocean without shores, and we don't know how to swim in its vastness.

Senseless people and fools don't understand that their success will not last (vv. 6–8). They don't know that the enemies of the Lord will squeak like defeated eagles. But the portion of the faithful is blessings, pearls, and precious jewels. They shall prosper in righteousness and bring forth fruit that destroys evil and its diseases.

O Lord, it is good to praise you every day. I praise you, for I see that my past is full of mercy and a love that does not compromise. I praise you while I taste your poured-out grace, the bread of the angels, and the harvest of heaven. I praise you when I hear about a wonderful future that is only one step away. I find in you a lasting joy, a spiritual awakening, free from slumber and distraction. So I am resolved to praise you today.

I want to be a palm tree in the land of the Lord (v. 12). I want to quench my thirst by drinking the cup of faith and sipping the water of your mercy. I will become a green tree bearing much fruit, and through my praise I will proclaim you to the nations, including Edom. The Lord is my Rock. Unlike Absalom, you do not rebel against truth or betray the covenant. I shall praise you today and every day.

~ Prayer from Psalm 93 ~

He is robed with majesty and sits on the throne (v. 1). His greatness is breathtaking! The everlasting one imprisons time in his palm (v. 2).

When Isaiah saw the Lord, he wept because of his own defilement. He recognized that he lived among unclean people. Even angels hid their faces when the Lord sat on his throne.

The Lion of heaven has come! He is clothed with majesty. John wept because all others failed, but the Lord succeeded. He had touched the untouchable and done the impossible when he sat on the throne. He has clothed himself with glory and demolished oppression.

The King of kings has come and has trodden down evil. He has crushed and obliterated oppression. The wolves of evil have howled, but the Lord has spoken with authority. At his word, all the tornados of evil and their garbage were swept away. They challenged him with their vices and blew the trumpet of battle. They lifted up their voices to spread illusions and fear. They stood shoulder to shoulder, advancing like a flood. But he came with the holiness of heaven and silenced and muzzled evil. The floods of sin and streams of murder dried up. The Lion of heaven has completely destroyed evil!

O Lord, be the King of my life, for my heart seeks your kingdom. Be my King every moment and in every breath.

~ Prayer from Psalm 94 ~

O Lord, evildoers pour out arrogant words (v. 3). Their utterances are rude (v. 4). They boast of iniquities and speak evil. They crush your people and humiliate your inheritance (v. 5). They kill the widow and put the orphan to death (v. 6). They are senseless, without any caution, and they are fools without understanding (v. 8). Thus they band together against the righteous and condemn the innocent to death (v. 21).

O Lord, judge the deeds of the arrogant (v. 1)! Announce good news to the humble. Rise against evildoers and stand against the people of iniquity (v. 16). Don't refuse the ones who listen to you; don't abandon the upright (v. 14). Show your mercy to those who call upon your name (v. 18). Comfort the anxious (v. 19).

Will the creator of the ear fail to hear the screams of his daughters and the cries of his sons? Will the maker of eyes fail to see the pain of those he loves (v. 9)? Will the fountain of justice fail to vindicate his oppressed people? Today you are my helper. You are the faithful one who comes to my aid (v. 17). O eternal rock, we seek your help. We plead for mercy from the Most Merciful One. Destroy the evil of the wicked, for you are the faithful lover.

~ Prayer from Psalm 95 ~

Come and let us sing for joy to the Lord! Let us shout aloud to the Rock of our salvation (v. 1). We enter into his presence with thanksgiving; we greet him with singing (v. 2). Let us know that he is the God of gods, and let us recognize the greatness of our God (v. 3). The deepest parts of the earth and the peaks of mountains are like dust on the balance scales before him (v. 4). He created heaven and earth and everything in them (v. 5). He shines light on every dark and gloomy place.

Come, let us be blessed and be a blessing before our Maker. Let our tongues sing praises. Our mouths shall not stop singing. Let all who complain and curse be silent. Let those who go astray and act sinfully stand still. Let those who quarrel and fight cease their aggression!

Let us instead bind our evil with the tears of holiness, and let us watch as the finger of the Lord silences and muzzles evil. He alone is the physician of the heart and the painter who draws our future. He is the shepherd, and we are the flock of a leader who does not oppress (v. 7). He is kinder than kindness and more beautiful than beauty. In his presence, our spirits breathe and inhale love. Our desire to praise him builds like a mountain.

Therefore, people of God, don't harden your hearts. Don't allow yourselves to become deaf and dumb (v. 8). Instead, praise and exalt our great God! He is merciful and strong. Don't choose to spend forty years in the wilderness, for the Lord poured out his anger on those wanderers (v. 11). Only those who choose him, those who exalt him and wake up dreaming about him, shall enter the land of heaven's promise and its eternal rest.

Prayer from Psalm 96

Praise the Lord with a new song! Sing to the God of all the earth (v. 1). Offer a new song (Pss 33:3; 40:3; 98:1; 144:9; 149:1; Isa 42:10). Sing every day and reflect on his victories. Exalt the Lord of lords and spread the good news of his salvation (v. 2). Do not cease from telling of his miracles or honouring the name of the Lord among the nations (v. 3). Our God is the greatest and most merciful being. He is the omnipotent one; therefore we shall praise him (v. 4)!

The nations are ignorant of the glory of God; so they worship idols (v. 5). Their song is old; do not dance to its melody. Evil accompanies its music; do not welcome their words into your ears. His mercy is new every morning; therefore rest in praising and believing in him.

The Lord alone creates a new heaven; therefore offer him your hearts. The King of heaven will give us a new land; therefore put off your hearts of stone. He shall grant us a new heart and a new spirit; therefore exult in the Lord!

But with this new creation, comes a new commandment to commit ourselves to love. When our tears drop like showers of rain, then we shall sing of the worthiness of the Lamb. O people of God, today is a day of praise! Therefore, praise him.

~ Prayer from Psalm 97 ~

Yahweh alone is the King of kings (v. 1). Justice and truth are the pillars of his throne (v. 2). The fire of his holiness burns all evil (v. 3). Lightning and thunder accompany his coming (v. 4). The mountains melt like wax before him (v. 5). His light is more intense than the sun, and all nations recognize that he owns the earth (v. 6). All false gods fall down before him (v. 7), but those who cling to Christ, the master of the universe, stand up; they guarantee their lives.

Those who cling to futile worldly things will encounter his wrath. What about you, O people of God? Let us acknowledge his authority. Let us rejoice and exult in his decrees (v. 8). Let us humble ourselves before him, for there is no limit to his greatness (v. 9). May we bow down today in the presence of our King and worship him. Let us love the King and hate evil. May we cast out fear and instead trust in the Lord. He is the keeper of his children (v. 10). Let us take off sadness and put on joy because of his presence. Let us serve the King of heaven and earth. Let his praise be our daily concern (v. 12).

~ Prayer from Psalm 98 ~

O Lord, I need a new song and a glorious hymn. I am tired of the songs of yesterday and this monotonous life. Let the rivers of praise flow and the dull life diminish! You alone are the Maker of wonders. You have a powerful arm (v. 1). You reveal your works, but I need both sight and insight (v. 2). You save and show mercy to my neighbours Muhammad, Moses, and Muneera. You are the saviour of Arabs, Jews, every country, and every island (v. 3).

O Lord, I need new words, for I long to sing a new poem. When I praise you, I see the walls of evil fall, with all humanity witnessing the miracle (Josh 6). I shall sing with Jehoshaphat before the invincible armies of evil (2 Chr 20). Let us open the doors of the prison with our prayers and our praises (Acts 12:3–12; 16:19–34). When we exalt the Lord, righteousness spreads, and sin flees.

O church, shout unto the Lord! Let all the earth sing words of wisdom (v. 4). The Lord is the King of kings. In his presence there is rest. He is the Lord of mercy, justice, and the right paths. Let us amass all the singers and their melodies; let the strings play and the music ring out. Let us dance and clap our hands, and let the beautiful choirs sing (v. 8)! Let our hearts, homes, churches, and countries praise the Lord, for praising him is a virtue.

O Lord, I declare that you are King, especially on evil days when I feel like a small boat in the eye of a hurricane. I shall praise you, magnify your name, and exalt you! I will feast on the new song, for it is delicious to my soul. Today I will cease complaining and instead become a nurturer of praise. Today I will sing a new song!

~ Prayer from Psalm 99 ~

The Lord reigns, therefore let the nations tremble. The earth shakes, for he is sitting amongst the cherubim (v. 1). Let all knees bow and let all lips praise his awesome name (v. 3)! The God of Jacob is the King of holiness, integrity, truth, and justice (v. 4).

O Lord, reveal your greatness before the eyes of human beings. Lift up the curtain that prevents us from seeing you. Grant the peoples of the world new eyes so that they can see your holiness. Make my life a telescope through which people can see your transcendence. But make me also a microscope through which they can experience the gift of your loving closeness. Let Arab nations taste your love, and restore the captives. At your feet, every wise person bows down.

Among your priests are Moses, Aaron, and the beloved Samuel (v. 6), from whom we learn to intercede for those who are wounded and humiliated by sin. The testimonies of the heroes of love and faith encourage us. They teach us the paths of righteousness.

You are the one who hears our prayers, who forgives our iniquities, and who changes our hearts. You are holy and can see into the depths of the heart. There is no blemish that can hide from your eyes. Sit on the throne of my life, of my church, and of my country!

Without you, wars spread everywhere. There are many kings spreading pain, sadness, and disasters. I will rebel against every other king except you, for you alone are the crucified King. You redeemed human beings with your death; thus the words of the prophets were fulfilled. Reign today and declare yourself our King, for our lives without you are like the setting sun.

I exalt you, O King of the universe, to be my King. I declare my loyalty to you, like my grandfather Job. I know you are able to do everything! It is not impossible for you to destroy evil and restore the captives. O my King, I offer my life to you. My heart is yours.

Prayer from Psalm 100

The joy of the Lord is my strength. Shouting unto the Lord is my candle in the midst of darkness. The wine of the Spirit is a drink from the Lord. In the midst of praising, a smile comes on my face. Everything is not okay, but I find my rest in praising God. My joy does not come through getting what I want, but by understanding the greatness of my King.

O Lord, you call me to enter a life of joy, so that my contentment is completed in you and by you. Shout to the Lord with gratitude and thanksgiving, O my soul (v. 1). At work and in the details of our daily lives, we serve a joyful God (v. 2).

Don't turn times of worship into dull seasons, but praise the Lord of holiness! At every moment, consider the sovereignty of God. Contemplate his fatherhood in every breath. Remember his care (v. 3). Don't sit on a bed of complaining and lie down in the presence of depression. Leave the land of darkness, the land of unhappiness, and run to the meadows of the Lord! When your heart sees the gates of praise, enter them (v. 4)! Bring a pen and list your blessings with gratitude. As the hymn says, even if the whole sea were ink and all the heavens were paper, there would not be enough ink and paper to write down all the blessings of God. Exalt his goodness, grace, love, and mercy.

Bless the Lord when you wake up and when you lie down. When we bless him, sadness and moaning flee. O my soul, don't embrace sadness but be encouraged by the promises of the Lord. O Lord, today I shall rejoice and laugh with the angels! My laughter shall be loud!

~ Prayer from Psalm 101 ~

The eyes of people are blinded, but the eyes of the Lord are alert. He sees that evildoers have imprisoned nations, killed children, and worshipped idols.

O God, you are the God of mercy and justice, and the Lord of your sheep (v. 1). I declare my loyalty to your justice with my song, my words, and my deeds. Evildoers oppress the weak, and good people are muzzled. As a result, evil grows stronger and remorse disappears. But I will pour out my heart before the Lord of justice until his sheep act with integrity.

I declare that my house is a house of justice. I shall not forget truth or be a coward (v. 2). I shall not abandon divine justice because I am afraid. I shall not turn a blind eye for personal benefit or for a bribe. The justice of humans has no eyes; it lives in utter darkness. But the mind of God is purer than snow.

O Lord, grant me on this earth the courage to spread truth, so that heaven cannot accuse me of being a coward. I shall declare that I don't endorse evil (v. 4), tolerate the arrogant (v. 5), or dwell with liars (v. 7). I declare war against oppression. I shall fight with all of my strength until the voices of evil are silenced (v. 8).

Oppression is my enemy, but those who believe in the Lord are safe. I will fight bitterness and put hatred to death everywhere and at all times as I cruise in my boat of love on the river of justice. The cross of our Lord is the foundation of justice and its fountain. There the river of justice overflows and the Lord scoops justice up with the cup of love. Then he gives it to all of us.

Prayer from Psalm 102

O Lord, depression has invaded my home. Sickness is wearing my clothes. Pain dwells in my heart. Do not hide your face from me (v. 2). My life is like the last pages of an old book; its paper is fragile. My bones are burning inside me (v. 3). Illness has sapped my courage and ruined my appetite (v. 4). I have forgotten to eat my bread. With every breath I hear my groaning, and I am reduced to skin and bones (v. 5). I am like the lonely desert owl inhabiting desolate places (vv. 6–7). Evildoers have multiplied against me, and my enemies despise me (v. 8). I have only ashes to eat, and my drink is mixed with my tears (v. 9). The waves of your anger have carried me away and cast me down (v. 10).

Do not hide your face from me. Please have mercy on me, for I became sick when my country suffered. Pain entered my heart when my people were humiliated. Evildoers ended my joy when they destroyed justice and massacred love. I beg you for mercy! Please listen to me! Come back to your home; be my King and the King of all people. Come back so the sun of compassion may shine again and the captives return. When you come back, the boys and girls of my people, who have become the children of death, will be redeemed (v. 20).

Let heaven shower mercy on us, for the rain of compassion heals. Won't you rebuild humiliated Zion so my people can join your church? Your absence has stabbed my heart and has silenced the praise of my country. The land of the cross cries out to you! Arab nations cry before you. Come, O Lord, and end the season of destruction so that we may begin to rebuild with love.

~ Prayer from Psalm 103 ~

O my soul, arise and get up! It is time for you to bless! Let my inner soul bless his holy name. Get up from the bed of forgetfulness and remember his blessings. Open your eyes, and don't ignore his many mercies. He forgives all your sins and rebukes sickness to heal you. He redeems your life from the pit, so remember his compassion and mercy. He gives his blessings with generosity, so approach his table of blessing. Lift up the cup of life and raise the cup of love! Enjoy the glances of the beloved and relish his care. It is time to give thanks.

Do not deny his great generosity. He does not forget the oppressed; therefore take heart. He does not overlook a child; therefore do not be lazy. He never fails; therefore contemplate his greatness.

Despite the powerful beasts that live within you, remember that the Lord is greater than your sin. Despite the enormous spread of evil in our land, cling to the mercies of God. His mercy will prevail, so rejoice! He has forgotten my sin, and my song has been born in the kingdom of love. It is time to give thanks. Do not stop praising the Lord of heaven.

Get up, and praise the goodness of Christ and his glorious cross. Through Christ you have become a person of royalty; enjoy your adoption! Today I urge you to bless; arise and get up!

～ Prayer from Psalm 104 ～

Y ou have robed yourself with light as if it is a garment (v. 2). You have clothed yourself with glory (v. 1). How great are your works! They are full of your wisdom. You have inhabited heaven and made it your home. You have ridden on the wings of the wind (v. 3). You have established earth on solid ground and have drawn the borders of the waters. You have created the stars and moons, and assigned times for the different planets. Indeed your works are full of wisdom. You have made springs burst out in the valleys and filled the heavens with brilliant lightning. With your thunder, you have rebuked your creation. You have quenched the thirst of the animals of the world and have taken care of the birds of the sky.

With great generosity, you have made provision for us. You have grown plants for the beasts of the field. You have brought forth bread from the earth for humans and have gladdened our hearts with wine. Our faces shine with oil. You have given us bananas and almonds. You are the Lord of every breath.

You have provided water for the smallest creatures as well as the largest. You have provided protection for the strongest creatures as well as the weakest. You have given the birds their nests and the hyrax their rocky shelters. You have fed the young lions and commanded the fish of the sea. You have provided food for all creation and poured out drinks for them. Heaven and earth are full of your generous gifts!

Every needy person receives your blessing, for your open hand does not withhold. With a loving heart, you have shown compassion. If your light turns to darkness, we can no longer live.

If you depart from our home, our hearts will be torn. But with your Spirit, we are recreated and the face of the earth is renewed. You embrace your sons with love and hug your daughters with compassion. I will sing and praise, for you have blessed us. How great are your works! They are full of your wisdom.

～ Prayer from Psalm 105 ～

Remember the wonders of God. O Lord, we are your people whom you protected from oppressors. You rebuked kings for our sake. You declared us to be your anointed ones and your prophets, so no one should abuse us. You shook heaven and earth for the sake of protecting us.

We remember your wonders when you fought against the enemies of your people. You turned their water into blood and killed their fish. You released frogs into the inner rooms of kings. You commanded flies and mosquitos to spread over their lands. Hail and flames of fire fell on their homes. All their trees shattered because of your wrath. The locusts ate their grass. All the first-born of their children died.

We remember your wonders, for you have brought your people out of the land of oppression. You protected our heads by providing clouds, and illuminated our nights with your light. We asked for meat, and you gave us quail. You satisfied us with the bread of heaven. You crushed the rock, and water gushed out for our sake.

Many years later, you sent your beloved; the only begotten came to our camp. In Nazareth, you declared the greatest news, and in Bethlehem our Messiah was born. He lived in Galilee, as our light and bread, but we killed him in Jerusalem. We hung him on a cross, but you forgave us. He rose from among the dead, then appeared to us; you poured your Spirit upon us. You transformed the world by our testimony.

O Lord, I am one of your people! Abraham is my father, and the blessed Mary is my hero. I follow in their footsteps. Like Paul, my heart aches because many are far from you; I pray for their salvation. You are the God of wonders, and your people need you today; thus I lift up a prayer for them and for myself. Strengthen me to obey you and to become like a Moses to my people, leading them to your blessing.

~ Prayer from Psalm 106 ~

I praise you because you are good. In the midst of distress, I give thanks unto the Lord. I beg for your compassion because you are merciful, and in the midst of my pain, I praise you.

We have sinned and done wrong, and we are guilty. We did not understand your wonders throughout our history. Instead, we complained, murmured, and grumbled. We were not mindful of your mercies. When we fell into the hands of the one who hates us, we did not seek your guidance. The enemy grabbed our necks, and we defiled your name. We created a golden calf and a molten image. We despised your greatness. We worshipped idols and moved away from your dwelling place. We sacrificed our boys and girls, pouring out their innocent blood. We became defiled by our deeds and works. We defiled the land of Canaan.

An earthquake devoured our leaders, Dathan and Abiram. We were under your discipline, and fire broke out around us. Moses and Aaron stood in the gap before you. Let Phinehas stand today so that the epidemic will not spread and your anger may be withdrawn.

O Lord, release us from the imprisonment of our sins. Set us free, so that our hearts may rejoice and praise you. Pardon our sins and conquer our iniquities with your forgiveness. O Lord our God, save us and purify us from our iniquities by the blood of your Son. We have sinned, as did our fathers, but today we rejoice in your pardon. We commit ourselves and our children to continually boast in the Lord and to praise him every day. Amen, and again, Amen.

～ Prayer from Psalm 107 ～

I got lost in the wilderness. I was hungry and thirsty. My soul was longing for a touch of comfort. But I was distant from you, in need of medication. And now I am completely exhausted. There is no way out. Yet I cry out to you, for I don't want to live as your enemy. You graciously respond. Then you offer me the water of heaven. Your words are like a balm that heals every sickness. When all the inhabitants of heaven and earth watch how you treat me, they praise your mercy and wonders.

I was shackled with humiliation and iron. I insulted the Lord of heaven, the one who is full of intense love. I rebelled against the council of the Most High and against his wise decrees. Therefore, I became tired and was in pain. Darkness invaded my life. I lived under its threat. But I cried out to you from my prison. Then you released me and broke the iron shackles. By your grace I departed from the land of darkness. You healed my heart and its arteries.

I praise you even in the midst of darkness, for you have sent me heavenly mail containing your promises. I praise you in the wilderness, the land of pain and sickness, before the gates of death, and in the midst of a tornado. I praise you when I am alone, because only you can transform the wilderness into a fountain of water. You conquer evil, sadness, and the waywardness of leaders. You are the one who feeds the hungry and guides the lost. You are a glorious light in the midst of darkness.

I cry out to the King of heaven on this day. I don't want to complain or point out our many troubles, but instead I want to praise God. I want to magnify the Lord, for he has shown the sons of Adam and the daughters of Eve his mercy and wonders.

➤ Prayer from Psalm 108 ➤

O Lord, I sing with my voice and spirit. My heart wants to magnify you. My eyes look at your work that blessed me yesterday. Because of your faithfulness and grace yesterday, my heart is steadfast today.

My heart is steadfast as I encounter trials, hardships, and even the devils of the world. I shall not neglect praising you even in the midst of wars. I shall not pause in magnifying you wholeheartedly. I will awaken the sun from its slumber with my praises. I shall declare a rising dawn full of worship and praise to the Lord of heaven. I will magnify you before the nations, and also before my friends and foes. I praise you in my joy and my distress. I will be clothed with praise outside my home, and when I converse with Shlomo, Ahmed, and Johnny.

I know that your mercy is higher than the mountains that penetrate the clouds. It is deeper than the valley that swallows the waters. It is a rock that cannot be destroyed by my evil or distress. Let my praises match your mercy! Let all the angels join in praising the King of heaven. Let our music and prayers be transformed into an acceptable perfume as we worship and offer our incense.

In the depths of the sea of praises, you speak to me and confirm your desire to sanctify me. I cannot be victorious without crucifying my sin. My praises will lead towards my sanctification and towards the victory of wisdom over my ignorance.

Praising you enlarges my vision and grants me the strength of heaven to do celestial deeds. It is a turning point as I move away from reacting to evil and instead become an agent of justice who challenges hatred with love. You empower me to conquer every evil, to take off my shoes in front of Edom and to wash my feet in Moab. Salvation is possible only by you, but I shall conquer evil by praising you. I shall win the battle against every foe, in spite of my fears and my own will. Today my heart is steadfast in praising you.

∼ Prayer from Psalm 109 ∼

O Lord! Declaring divine judgment is not less spiritual than offering praise. Genuine spirituality is not limited to forgiveness and divine love. Indeed, justice and truth demand a heavenly response.

My prayer is not rooted in revenge, nor is it a call for hatred. My anger is not against humans, but against the absence of humanity. I do not seek to pronounce a curse on them but to reveal their cursed eternal destiny. My anger is based on your fiery holiness and does not depend on my selfish inclinations. It is prophetic anger. At its core dwells eternal love, as well as a call to repent and rehumanize ourselves.

In such a spirit, I plead that you shut satanic mouths! Terminate their sharp words and defuse their poisonous speeches. Destroy ISIS and remove them from our daily news. Judge the killers of children and declare your justice before those who transgress the commandment of love. Don't accept hypocritical prayers, but declare hypocrites guilty. Expel them from your presence.

One divine curse is more compassionate than all satanic blessings. Any so-called blessings that encourage people to participate in sin are utter evil. Let people suffer the consequences of their sins before it is too late. Clothe them with your curse and let them drink the cup of pain like drinking water. In the harshness of your punishment, may hell-bound people wake up! May they repent when they taste the judgment of God! May they know that your hand supports your church and spreads eternal blessing!

~ Prayer from Psalm 110 ~

All of us are weak in comparison to celestial power. All of us are ignorant compared to your wisdom; therefore I will magnify you and praise you. I will not act before sitting at your right hand for guidance. In the midst of a sea of worries, I will sit in the boat of patience. I shall sit at your right hand where divine strength, eternal wisdom, and victory over hardships are found. I will sit at your right hand where my heart is moved and my faith is grown, and there the enemy will honour me.

When I sit at your right side, your hand moves and your strength appears. At your right hand, there is youth, beauty, benediction, and the perfume of blessing. There is the dawn of love and the adornment of holiness.

Draw me to the presence of your right hand. Embrace me with your left arm, for I have lost my compass. I have forgotten my geography. My enemies have multiplied, and so I need to behold the Lion of Judah sitting at your right hand. At your right hand, I hear the voice of thunder, and the Lord appears at my right hand.

In Christ, I sit at your right hand and my identity is transformed. I become a priest who can communicate with the words of God. When I sit at your right hand, my position is elevated. I become like Melchizedek. My problems become insignificant, and evil becomes like a bug under our feet. At your right hand, I see the weakness of kings and the crushing of evil's head. At your right hand, I drink the water of life and find rest and honour.

Lead me today to enter into the presence of your right hand. Lead me to sit there. Sitting is the sign of change; it is the beginning of God's miracles in my life, as well as in the lives of those around me. Jesus sat at your right hand after he conquered death; our Messiah sat at your right hand. Then you poured out your Spirit. When he sits at your right hand, the final judgment is one step away. I am in him at your right hand. I shall not move as long as I am alive.

~ Prayer from Psalm 111 ~

I praise you using every known alphabet and colour. My lips draw thankfulness and gratitude with vibrant words. I sing melodies to you in my house, in my inner thoughts, and in the midst of the righteous. How great are your deeds! Your mercies overshadow the whole world. You honour human beings and spread holy joy as you establish justice in every moment of time.

Today, I remember your goodness and wonders. I celebrate your friendship, refusing to deport your compassion and mercy to the land of forgetfulness. You have saved us from evil. You have fed us quail, manna, and pomegranates. You have taught us holiness, patience, and hope as you led us to the land of Canaan. You have made promises and have demonstrated impeccable faithfulness. History testifies that you have never lied to an angel or to a human being. Your words are more precious than gold, more glorious than the brightest sun, and are full of compassion. You fight for the sake of spreading righteousness. You sanctify your children. You shepherd them. You save them from evil tongues and from teeth that are like knives.

O Holy God, I shall praise you! All souls and bodies bow down before you. Honouring you is the greatest wisdom; help me to become an expert in it. I praise you today wholeheartedly, and I sing to you with gratitude and thanksgiving!

～ Prayer from Psalm 112 ～

We bless you today because you bless us every day. Your blessing moves every heart, even hearts of granite. You are the source of every blessing, not money, power, or human beings.

Blessed are those whom you bless. They obey your Word and study it without getting bored (v. 1). Their descendants will have a great reputation because of their heritage (v. 2). Their house is full of celestial gifts, and by the grace of God, their righteousness shall forever prevail (v. 3). Their life is the embodiment of mercy and compassion; in the midst of darkness, there is light and vision (v. 4). Their money is a gift from God. By the grace of the Most High, they show compassion and share their wealth (v. 5). Their remembrance is forever, and they are not hurt by the sun or by rain (v. 6). Their hearts are steadfast in trust, and because of the Lord, they do not fear any news (v. 7). They have courageous hearts that conquer fear and are not afraid to listen or look (v. 8). They stand like a lion until they see evil depart. They are smart in their investments. In addition, they are smarter than many people. After they are paid, they are generous in giving to the poor and in spreading goodness (v. 9). Their hearts don't turn into stone. They are not content with the blessing of receiving; they care for the needy and the poor. They hear the cries of the distressed.

O Lord, turn me into a channel of your mercy so I can stand against evildoers. Empower me to stand with the oppressed and humiliated. Turn me into a channel of blessing for every needy person until the world knows that the generosity of the Lord dominates and overwhelms humankind. Today is a day of giving. So let us present our gifts joyfully and give generously in order to conquer our selfishness, self-indulgence, and greed.

~ Prayer from Psalm 113 ~

With all of my heart I praise you. I am no longer Pharaoh's slave. Today I am yours! I was imprisoned by my sin, but you liberated me. I was in debt and condemned, but you justified me. I was sad, but you gave me joy. I praise you!

I have found none who are as faithful as you, or as kind, or as just, or as loving. I praise you! When I was a child, you were with me. In my hunger, you fed me. When I was tired, you took care of me. In my ignorance, you gave me guidance. I praise you!

I woke up and found you waiting for me. With your love and compassion, you embraced me. I praise you! All day long you empower me, and then you tuck me into my bed. I praise you! I am your spoiled child, and your love overwhelms me. From the moment I wake up until the moment I sleep, I praise you.

The King of kings receives me, and the creator of the universe offers me a seat in his presence. With his glances and many gifts, he honours me. I praise you!

When I accept your plan, celebrate your attributes, and spread your justice and mercy, I am praising you. With gratitude, prayers, and action, I praise you. When I was in a bottomless pit, you came down to me. When I was sitting in dirt and garbage, you did not hesitate to come to me and lift my downcast head. I applaud your sacrifices and praise you. Your presence changes everything! You lifted me up from failure and disgrace; then you offered me a seat among the nobles of your people. I praise you!

With your touch, you have replaced emptiness and worry with the fruit of the Spirit. I have become a mother by your mercy; because of your generosity, I now have many children. I applaud your deeds and praise you!

Today and every day, my heart is thankful, for you have filled my life with your grace. Today is a day of praise. Glory is to you alone.

~ Prayer from Psalm 114 ~

O God of freedom, you alone can free us from slavery. Without freedom, we suffer oppression, subjugation, and bigotry. Without freedom, we encounter every day a new dictator, a Pharaoh who slaughters our children and humiliates our women. Without freedom, we have no names and no legal rights, not even the right to humane treatment. We are surrounded by checkpoints, prisoners of war, the crushed, the broken-hearted, refugees, orphans, and controversy. Without freedom, the fear, hatred, and darkness of evildoers dominate.

But the Saviour came! Evil leaped up to escape; the wicked retreated and quivered before the God of freedom. You brought your people out of Egypt. You divided the sea and shook the eternal mountains. Now declare your commitment to end oppression and challenge all kinds of sin, including all Pharaoh-like regulations!

Yet merely breaking our shackles is not enough to give us freedom; we also need to see the birth of a heavenly civilization, one of holiness, celestial heroism, and victory over every obstacle that prevents the coming of freedom.

Before we can stand on the mountain of victory, before we can conquer the devilish schemes, we must walk in the valley of the shadow of death. O Lord, it is not enough to loathe the evil of Pharaoh; we must also follow you wholeheartedly. We must watch you break the iron chains of evil. We follow you, for danger with you is better than the peace of slavery.

O Lord of freedom, we follow you! You alone are genuine freedom, a freedom that starts first in the heart, then the tongue. It liberates both the soul and the body. O Lord may your kingdom come, a kingdom of freedom! Turn the wilderness and slavery of our countries into fountains of divine blessing, by the miraculous power of heaven.

∽ Prayer from Psalm 115 ∽

We are a minority, surrounded by aggressive religions, and many publicly challenge your Holy Trinity. They shout, "Where is your Messiah?" Where is the Lord of eternity? Persecution encircles us, along with brutal killing. Some think that God supports ISIS (Islamic State of Iraq and Syria), and others turn the name of Jesus into a Jewish curse. We are surrounded by distress and hardship! We are attacked because we are Christians.

Why? Why O Lord, do we have to face this disaster and hardship? Aren't you merciful? Why don't you have mercy on your children during our time in the wilderness and in the valley of the shadow of death? Aren't you faithful? Won't you deliver us from evil conspiracies? We have become disgraced slaves, even though we worship the God of truth, honour, glory, and freedom!

You have delivered us from Pharaonic shackles. By your cross, you have opened the gates of eternity. Our names have been written in your book. Thus our disgrace and weakness is a celestial disgrace!

Many worshippers have created heartless and senseless gods who can't even see. They have abandoned the true creator. Like their gods, they have no eyes or ears and their hearts are made of flint. But we have committed ourselves to praise you and to trust your divine wisdom. We know that praising and trusting the resurrected Lord is the key to eternal pleasures. You are the Lord of all blessings. Human or satanic dams will not prevent the flow of your blessings. Today is a day of trust and praise, despite the fiery tongues of evil.

Prayer from Psalm 116

I have encountered hellish hardships and have been suffocated by ropes of death (v. 3). I am suffering from distress and sadness, but I have called upon the name of the Lord (v. 4). I have humbled myself before the God of compassion, and by his grace he delivered me (vv. 4–6). I have been humiliated and confused, like Jonah in the belly of the fish. I cried out to the Lord, for my joy had been depleted. I cried out to the Lord because so many people have lied and distorted things (v. 11).

In the graveyard, I discovered the cup of salvation placed on a divine table (v. 13). After I had fasted and humbled myself, the Lord gave me a drink of joy and clothed me with purple and sapphires. When the righteous are taken to heaven, it is precious in the eyes of the Lord (v. 15). His compassion leaves me speechless.

You have loosened my chains and have torn death to pieces, declaring your greatness. You have delivered my eyes from the tyranny of tears. I praise you wholeheartedly and with all of my voice. I have been shaken by hardships, but because of you, my life has become full of Sabbath and rest. I sacrifice to you with praise, and I adorn myself with oil and joy. I magnify and thank you. I praise you and declare the end of heaven's silence with my praises. I praise you because you alone conquer lying, evil, oppression, and every idol.

Today I stand in the midst of your people. In your dwelling place I declare that I am not hated but loved! I shall fulfil my vows and shall not lie. Today is a day of thanksgiving and a day of fulfilling vows. It is a day carved in holiness and faithfulness.

∽ Prayer from Psalm 117 ∽

Before me is a psalm that is small in size but big in its influence. The mind of God and his will can appear in few or in many words.

The Lord's praise is not limited by bigotry, sectarianism, language, or ethnicity. The people of Argentina, Bahrain, Palestine, China, and the islands of the Grenadines are all his creatures. All nations without exception are his vision. Men, women, children, and the elderly are his people. The call, "Praise the Lord all you nations," goes out to all. So does the message, "Honour him, all you peoples."

When we are united with God, we are united with each other, and his aims are fulfilled. His season is every morning and every evening, and the sun of his faithfulness shines every second. His faithfulness is forever and ever. His loving kindness is for all nations. He embodied love before the heavens and earth existed.

His loving kindness extends to every poor person, every sinner, every despised human, every evildoer, and everyone who perishes! His grace appeared before the greatest evildoers; his plan appeared before crowds of sinners, from Adam to the last human being. It is the plan of mercy, of grace, of faithfulness. It is the plan of the love of the cross. It is the plan of the victory of grace over sin. His resurrection is the plan in which he overcomes death.

The Lord does not only call the nations to praise him, but he also makes them his own family. He grants them his Spirit, and his Messiah embodied his righteousness, love, and holiness before them. On this day I praise the Lord. I pray and seek the salvation of all nations. I seek the unity of the people of God and the fulfilment of their mission to the whole world.

~ Prayer from Psalm 118 ~

Perhaps I cannot give anything, but I can give thanks in everything. Therefore I command you, my soul, to stop complaining. Instead, start praising the Lord, whether it is summer or winter.

It is good to thank those who treat us well, but it is much better to thank the Lord of goodness and faithfulness. His goodness is without limits; it does not depend on us, it does not change with time, and it is void of deceit.

When I discover the depths of my corruption, I need to remember the mercy of the creator. His mercy is eternal and is stronger than any catastrophe. Let us therefore praise the Lord, for his loving kindness is forever.

To take refuge in the Lord is better than depending on leaders or even physicians. In the name of the Lord I shall fight evil and all those who abuse us. I will suffer, but I am not afraid, for I trust in the Lord. With him I shall find mercy, success, and joy.

Even if I become a rejected stone, I need to remember that in God's design for salvation, the standard of choosing stones is different from ours. Many evildoers and enemies rose up against the stone of heaven.

I lift up my prayers, as if I am in a desert without water. His mercy comes down like rain, and my pastures become green. The Lord, through the Messiah, has opened the gates of righteousness, and I no longer have to retreat. Because of his mercy, today is a day of salvation and glory. Today is a day of praise unto the heavenly Saviour, the one who created men and women. Praise the Lord for he is good, and his loving kindness is forever.

∽ Prayer from Psalm 119 ∽

Your Word is a sea of words. With the ebb of the tide, praises increase, and with the inflow, laments are revealed. Your Word is like a river of light in the midst of darkness. It guides every stray person. It creates revivals. Your Word is like rain that quenches the thirst of every person under heaven who is thirsty for righteousness. Your Word is the fountain of truth, the well of grace, and the channel that leads to the bosom of God, even in the midst of hardship. Your Word is like a waterfall that washes away our corruption and cleanses our spirits from evil stains. In the midst of hardship, your Word is like snow on a hot summer day. You cover us with protective clouds before the burning sun of your holiness.

Today I shall drink the word of life. I will be transformed into a stream of wisdom that cannot be contained by oceans. Do not make me like the Dead Sea where the inflowing living waters become dead. My sin and laziness destroy the impact of your word in my life. Faith without works is dead. Words and faith without love are futile. O Lord, don't make me like the Red Sea, which does not understand except when struck by the staff of Moses, the same stick that was used against Pharaoh. I want to be like the Sea of Galilee that produces fish. Those fish were blessed by the one who fed the crowds with only two fish and five loaves. Make me like the Mediterranean, which carried the ambassadors of the Word of God. Through prayers, support, and encouragement, the Word of God reaches to all continents.

Today I quench my thirst with your Word, for it is the key to many blessings. I have treasured your words in my heart so that I might not sin against you. I don't want to become like evildoers or like hellish people. Your Word is the water bottle that I always carry, for I shall not survive in the wilderness without it. Your Word is the most precious thing in my day, and the best thing that I write about in my diary.

～ Prayer from Psalm 120 ～

O Lord, I am tired of the journalists who hate peace (v. 6). They rush to war, but I am a man of peace (v. 7). So I will start my adventure towards you with a dream in which I anticipate the coming of your kingdom. I dream of a Middle East in which I eat breakfast in Jerusalem, lunch in Beirut, and dinner in Syria. I drive my car to Iraq, to the Gulf, and then enter Africa, all in the same car. I dream of a Middle East in which people choose their own religion without fear. I dream of a Middle East in which there is no bigotry, radicalism, and hatred. I dream of a Middle East in which all human beings are equal, whether they wear a hijab, a keffiyeh, or a kippah. I dream of a Middle East in which Jews love Arabs and seek to uphold their rights, a Middle East in which Arabs love Jews. I dream of a Middle East without poverty, hatred, wars, or massacres. I dream of peace, peace with God and with all our neighbours, peace with self and with angels. I dream of a Middle East without weapons, without traffic jams, without pollution, without discrimination because of gender, religion, age, or weight.

My dream is not an illusion, but a step forward as I follow Jesus Christ, the prince of peace. My dream is not something that can be fulfilled in a moment; it is a celestial kingdom that comes through many generations and many sacrifices, prayers, and tears. Before the dawn, there is darkness; before joy, sadness has its victory; before laughing, weeping dominates; before the dominance of the kingdom of God, the kingdom of the devil reigns.

O Lord! May your kingdom come and your will be done on earth as it is in heaven! May your kingdom come through my words, thoughts, decisions, and relationships! Turn me into a peacemaker.

～ Prayer from Psalm 121 ～

In the valley of pain and amid the curved streets of rejection, I refuse to focus on myself, to look upon my worries and weaknesses. Instead, I shall lift up my eyes to the mountains. I don't look to them out of self-pity or fear, but out of faith and hope, and with the assurance that the Lord is my helper. I lift up my eyes to see the future and to feel the support of the divine hand. I lift up my eyes to see the power of God that is greater than the chains of time. I lift up my eyes because I want to see heavenly promises and eternal characteristics. I want to see the wakeful God who watches over his people and who is able to stop every kind of evil. I want to sleep knowing that God is vigilant, watching over me. I want to rid myself of blindness or myopic vision. Thus, I lift up my eyes to see you alone.

With my gaze, I seek your help; my glance is my prayer and cry. I need to stop looking at the slippery ground, the burning sun, and the coming evil. Instead, I want my glance to embrace the glance of God. Let me be mindful of God's protection. Let me understand that I am your treasure whom you keep safe from every corruption. Then I can make you the treasure for which I give up everything.

You are my refuge in the face of my soul's corruption and when I am surrounded by devils, fools, danger, traps, and conspiracies. I shall go to Jerusalem with my face fixed on you, even though all the demons of the world are trying to stop me. All the forces of evil cannot change my path. Disease and even death cannot prevent me from going. My ability to continue is not due to my strength, but yours. The strong one protects me.

My guarantee is not found in money, intelligence, or friends. It is found in the Lord. Today, I declare that you alone are my eternal protector and my keeper.

～ Prayer from Psalm 122 ～

Let us go to the house of the Lord, for it is full of joy (v. 1). In the presence of God our bodies are refreshed, as well as our souls and spirits. In his presence, we find rest, love, and success. In his presence, gloominess changes to laughter and mourning ends. In his presence we encounter others who praise and spread love as well as goodness.

The followers of the Lord come from every group and background. All of them declare that losing the gold of the world for the sake of God's name is the best profit. We are all one body; we stand together as we praise him. When evil comes, our united prayer is the best weapon against it.

Justice dwells in the presence of God; righteousness lies down in the midst of his people. There we see through the eyes and hear through the ears of heaven. We understand that the church stands against the darkness of the world as a lamp full of light.

O church of the Lord, I love you. You are the wings that help my spirit to fly. You elevate me to a position of better understanding, deeper peace, and joy. May the peace of your leaders and those who defend you multiply! May the people of peace and forgiveness rest in you! I pray for your prosperity, for you are my mother, my refuge, my joy, and my pasture. You nurse me with goodness, clothe me with understanding, and fight the lion as well as the alligator for my sake. May there be peace in your castles. May your pain end and your wounds heal!

O Lord, I pray today for the peace of the local and the global church. I pray for the ones who love the church, its members, its sons and daughters. Grant to all of them your benediction; open the gates of blessing, for the keys are found only in your hand.

~ Prayer from Psalm 123 ~

I lift up my eyes to the one who dwells in the heavens (v. 1). I lift up my eyes as Abraham lifted his when he wanted to see the eternal promise and seed. I lift up my eyes to count the stars of heaven, believing that you are a generous God. Like Isaiah, I raise my eyes to contemplate the power of the Most High. Like Nebuchadnezzar, I lift up my eyes to you. Then my mind is restored and I can bless the Lord of heaven, the Most High.

Before a stinking grave, I lift up my eyes to the Lord of everlasting life. Like Jesus, I lift up my eyes, asking that all people know the true God. When I meet a mute or deaf person, I lift up my eyes to the Lord of heaven. When I need bread and fish, with a thankful heart I raise my eyes. Like Stephen, I bow down on my knees. Then I lift up my eyes to see heaven open up in the midst of a bloody age. On the fields of Samaria, I raise my eyes to see a great harvest in which Arabs and Jews are saved. I lift up my eyes to be transformed and to become a divine tool for changing the oppressor and for helping the oppressed and the poor.

Like the eyes of servants looking towards their masters and maids towards their ladies, so my eyes will be lifted up to God, seeking mercy and compassion (v. 2). Today I will not look backward like the wife of Lot. I will not stare blindly like the servant of Elisha who did not see the angels of God. Unlike Asaph, I will not look at the strength of evildoers. But like John at Patmos, I will turn towards the voice that speaks to me, in order to behold your greatness. O God who lives in the heavens, I lift up my eyes to you.

~ Prayer from Psalm 124 ~

Had not the Lord intervened, Sarah, Rebekah, Rachel, the wife of Manoah, Hannah, and Elizabeth would have remained without children. Had not the Lord intervened, Israel would have stayed a slave to Pharaoh and the hardships would have continued. Had not the Lord intervened, Esau would have killed Jacob, Joseph would have died in exile, and Moses would have given up because of the many complaints. Had not the Lord intervened, Israel would have died in the wilderness, suffering from hunger, thirst, and snakebites. Had not the Lord intervened, our portion would have been the sword of Sihon and Balak. Curses would have destroyed us. Had not the Lord intervened, we could not have survived Ai, the evil of the people of Canaan, or Goliath. Had not the Lord intervened, the followers of Baal would have completely destroyed the people of God; Elijah would have failed and died. Had not the Lord intervened, Sennacherib would have destroyed the work of God, and we would not have seen divine judgment and God-sent plagues. Had not the Lord intervened, Daniel and three other young men would not have survived, and Jonah would not have come out of the belly of the fish, he would not have prevailed against the powerful currents in the depth of the sea.

Had not the Lord intervened, evil would long ago have put out the light of the church, and God's sons and daughters would have become extinct. But the trap has been broken, and we are free from the power of curses. The Maker of the heavens is our helper! The snare is broken, so I will not fear the wrath of people, the flood of evil, and the teeth of the devourer. I shall not be afraid during the day or even in my deepest sleep. On this day, we bless the Lord of the cross, the giver of freedom, and the creator of heaven and earth.

~ Prayer from Psalm 125 ~

O Lord, I trust in you. Such trust brings many blessings. Without you, my life is full of worry and gloom. But with you, it is an exciting adventure! Without trust in you, I am unhappy and impoverished. But when I rely on you, I become like Mount Zion. I am not moved by either a breeze or a great storm.

The Lord of the universe dwells in me; he has granted me both sight and insight. The Lord of love, truth, and forgiveness lives in my dwelling place. Before his greatness, everything else is insignificant. You have anointed kings in Zion and have made your blessings flow like a fountain. The nations of the earth seek you in Zion, and many peoples make pilgrimages there. It is there that wars will end. Every lamb will find its pasture in Zion, for you are a wall of fire around it; your skilled hand protects it. As Jerusalem is surrounded by mountains, so the Lord surrounds his people day and night, during seasons of light or darkness. Neither a wolf nor a fox shall approach Zion. No evil will spread its confusion there. Swords, murder, evil, and malice will fail before Zion. Every eye in it will sleep well.

O Lord, bless those who trust in you, whether in seasons of hardship or pleasure. Today, I am like Mount Zion. I proclaim your presence, sovereignty and peace, and your protection of your people. I declare that trusting in you brings bountiful blessings.

~ Prayer from Psalm 126 ~

Slavery is over, and its chains are broken! The Lord has ended exile and restored the dream of Zion. Misery, hardship, and the gloom of unhappiness are finished. Instead of wretchedness, tongues are singing unto the Lord. Our mouths are full of laughter, a holy laughter! It is time to be proud of Zion and its people. The Lord has magnified his work, and every guitar plays its chords. The joys of freedom, holiness, love, and unity dwell in Zion. Rivers of blessings water its land.

Gone is the toil of sowing seeds, for today is a day of harvest. God has answered the prayers of many and has treasured their tears. The seeds of love have penetrated the land of rebellion, rejection, and hatred. Every seed we planted in such fields was accompanied by a tear, and the Lord heard our cries. With every step, our feet encountered thorns and thistles, but on our way back we harvested great rewards.

The time of exile, fear, and surrender before the enemy is over. It is time for the resurrection of Zion, for God has sent Jesus to liberate her and break her chains. God has sent his Spirit and filled the children of Zion. The Most High has filled its gates with saints.

Today I shall walk in Zion and laugh and enjoy its laughter. I proclaim the end of slavery and the dawn of Zion's liberation, as well as mine.

Prayer from Psalm 127

Had the Lord not saved me I would have remained a hellish person. Had the Lord not taken care of me as an infant, death would have been my portion. Had the Lord not given me food and drink, woe would have been unto me. Had he not guarded my home and guided me, waywardness would have been my lot. Had he not comforted me in my distress, anxiety would have overwhelmed me. Had the Lord not been my friend, misery would have been my companion. Had the Lord not intervened, failure would have been my partner. Had the Lord not kept my mouth from gossip, my tongue would have become a burning fire. Had the Lord not shielded my eyes from sin, my glances would have embraced evil. Had the Lord not protected my heart with his holy word, regret would have been my bedmate.

Without the Lord my work is futile, and my life is in vain; my family and children are in vain. Without him, all my thoughts, work, words, and accomplishments are pointless. But with him I am truly blessed, even when I sleep. With him, I find pleasure, grace, and satisfaction, even as I fast. I find with him my salvation, rest, and peace. With him, I am with my blessed family all the days of my life. Many photos of sons and daughters adorn my heart and walls. The fruits of holiness and love fill my pages.

Unless the Lord builds the house, the workers work in vain (v. 1). But when the Lord builds the house, how great is my joy! Today, I deliver into your hands my house, my life partner, and my children.

~ Prayer from Psalm 128 ~

O Lord, I affirm your promise to share goodness with everyone who fears you and walks in your ways (v. 1). But I have planted, laboured, and am now tired. Please grant me to eat from the fruit of my labour, for you alone are my King and owner (v. 2).

I rejoice in your promise to bless me with a fruitful, virtuous woman and with children. Her laugh is like a pleasant vineyard (v. 3). I take hold of your promise to bless me with a child; like an olive plant, he spreads blessing (v. 4). I claim your promise that I shall see my grandchildren and live long days protected from the destroyer (v. 6).

All day long, I proclaim your promise that I shall see the success of Jerusalem and the people of God, for you will always be the great blesser (v. 5). I affirm your promise that I shall live in the peace of Christ, the love of God, and the fellowship of the Holy Spirit because Christ shed his blood for me on the cross. I claim your promise that I will be richly blessed by the Lord of heaven and earth. With your good gifts, I will fight evil.

Today, I shall be encouraged by your promises, and be renewed. My joyful prayer will be full of thanksgiving. I shall thank a joyful God who confirms the blessing and the good fortune of all who cling to the path of righteousness.

～ Prayer from Psalm 129 ～

O my God, I believe in you in the midst of my distress. When I am surrounded by darkness and when glitter falls away, I will cling to the Lord of heaven. Evildoers have multiplied, but you shall continue to be my dearest friend.

I live now in a tunnel of pain. The smoke of worry is in every breath I inhale. Evildoers ploughed me down and turned my back into a road for their dirty feet. I have encountered hardship since I was young. But you have been my close companion and are closer than a brother. You have freed me. You have broken the chains of evil with your mercy and deep love. Through your goodness and love, you have transformed me from a traitor into a lover and partner.

I am Zion, your people. Therefore let opposition, hatred, nagging, and battle cries cease! Let your love defeat the forces of evil and their demons. Let every inappropriate deed fail. Let the sun of your love shine and the gathering of evildoers dry up like dead grass under a burning sun.

May the season of blessing come to us! Let the doors of heaven swing wide, making its markets accessible to us. Then I shall find goodness, blessings, heavenly pearls, and precious celestial stones. Then I will linger in the garden of divine pleasure like a butterfly tasting the nectar of roses.

Heavy labour is the lot of those who hate Zion, but those who love Christ's people will have wings of faith that help them fly. We can soar over the pains of life and see the myriad of angels who welcome us with a standing ovation. Bless us, O Lord! We bless you and your people, whether in a season of hardship or pleasure.

~ Prayer from Psalm 130 ~

When we are in the dark places of deep pain and intense hardship, a strong faith is born, as well as a cry that penetrates the heavens. O Lord, listen for my cry! Let your ears hear my supplication!

In the deep, dark world, I have learned to wait upon the Lord of blessings. I have waited for you, living on dry crumbs, all the while desiring a feast of love. I have been hoping day and night; my eyes have not slept or slumbered. I am a poor person knocking at your door, seeking mercy and redemption. Please grant me your greatest gifts.

I am sinful and guilty. My feet are sunken into the mud of deep darkness. Clearly, I am not fit to stand before you, but you hold the solution for you grant forgiveness to sinful and guilty people! Forgive us our debts, and we will also forgive the debts of those who have sinned against us.

I am a paralyzed person, lying on a bed of woe. I am an adulteress surrounded by violence, oppressive deeds, words, and leers. I am a sinful woman of many tears, begging at your feet with kisses of repentance. I owe ten thousand talents. I am one of a people who killed every joy and slaughtered the blood of holiness in the wilderness of evil and complaint.

Forgive my guilt, for I have sinned in word, in deed, and in disregarding you. I have multiplied my sins. I cannot change the past, but your forgiveness can change my future and can help me encounter the miracles of God. Today, I pray that the pure blood of Christ will cover me as I seek your forgiveness.

⌣ Prayer from Psalm 131 ⌣

O Lord, examine my heart. Out of the heart come thoughts that shape my life and determine my path. The dirt of my heart muddies the fountain of my words with evil. This poisonous dirt is full of the venom of arrogance and pride, which declares me guilty and destroys my innocence.

O Lord, protect my eyes, for they are the mirror that reflects the condition of my heart. When my heart is healthy, my eyes are clear. Ah, my heart. I will not seek greatness and prominence, but will instead seek to please the Lord. I don't want to be a star in heaven, but a candle in the dark spot that God has entrusted to me.

After I muted my thoughts, I heard the voice of my master. His voice came like a trumpet full of divine declaration. It came like a land in which wisdom and strength grow.

O Lord, make me like a long-necked giraffe so that I have enough time to think about my words before saying them. Grant me ears like rabbits to enable me to listen when I am silent. My words are like birds of prey that destroy, but you can make my lips like a strong iron cage; with great determination, I can prevent the birds from flying.

I have not chosen the path of warriors who fight their opponents, but the path of an infant in the bosom of his mother. O Lord, in your bosom my silence declares the death of my sinful words, thoughts and dreams. I cling to you so that your dream becomes mine. Today, I shall quiet myself, even in the storms and hardships of life. I shall discover God and hear his voice. Then my hope will grow in the midst of my silence.

⌣ Prayer from Psalm 132 ⌣

O Lord, I commit myself to seek your presence and to build your house, which is more important than building my house. Your comfort is more precious than my sleep. I seek to praise your name, adopt your values, and spread your plan. Your name is far more important than mine. Your wishes come before mine.

O Lord, I commit myself to gathering your sons and daughters around you. Your presence is more important than my meetings. Pleasing you is far more essential than pleasing myself. Crowning you as king is more imperative than my job.

For your sake, I will leave my palace and sing loudly to magnify your name. For the sake of your servants, Abraham (Gen 26:4) and David (v. 10), you have blessed us, but for the sake of your son Jesus, your blessings have overflowed us! O Lord, you have matched my commitment with a great sacrifice. You delivered your Son to be crucified. My sacrifices are like dust in comparison to your great deeds. Not only did you send your many blessings but you even came yourself!

O Lord, Earth's blessings are rooted in heaven, and you have generously opened your hand, granting us your gifts. You have built a house of stone, and by your presence it has become a place of miracles. When you entered your earthly house, you transformed weakness into strength, mortality into immortality. Today, I commit myself to build your house and to seek your presence.

~ Prayer from Psalm 133 ~

W hen brothers and sisters meet together, they embody the unity of the family (v. 1); our joy and delight multiplies. We see Jacob embracing Esau after many years of alienation. We see Joseph pouring tears on the neck of Benjamin and the rest of his brothers despite their betrayal. We see divided kingdoms merging and bitter hearts defeated.

We who come from every tribe and every tongue are united in love. The perfume of divine grace and the rainbow of mercy clothe us. We love this heavenly fellowship where we enter the dwelling place of the Lord. There we discover that our high priest has engraved our names on his chest! He is a priest forever. He prays for our unity and intercedes with powerful supplication that ends division (v. 2).

His blessing is poured down on all of us, like the waters of Hermon that turn us into green trees (v. 3). It fills our land with love and unity. It restores the prodigal son and the lost sheep. It fills our bellies with the water of life and our mouths with genuine laughter. Without unity, love, and family, blessing is absent. But when we unite with Christ and with each other, the blessing of the Lord will be strong and everlasting. O Lord, I pray today for the unity of the people of God, the sons of the great King and the daughters of the divine family.

Prayer from Psalm 134

Bless the Lord with your thoughts, words, and deeds. Bless the Lord with your voices, hands, and feet. O servants of the Lord, bless the Lord!

He is the Lord of the world. He loves, redeems, liberates, heals, and does the greatest deeds. He does not slumber or sleep. So let us stand before him at night (v. 1). Let us exalt the Lord of peace. Let us praise the one whose is unlike any other. Let us enter the presence of God and break the chains and shackles by our praise. Let every hand be lifted up (v. 2), let every foot stand (v. 1). Yes, every paralyzed leg shall stand! Every shackled hand will be freed in praise and in celebration.

How great art thou, O Maker of heaven! You have created an earth adorned with valleys and mountains (v. 3). Indeed, you have created heaven and earth. You have given many generations your grace and mercy.

When I bless you, I am blessed a thousand-fold by you; you take away all my burdens. I shall exalt you, praise your work, and celebrate your attributes. I will stop arguing and start blessing. I shall bless the servants of the Lord and his people every day. You have called me to bless and to be blessed by an omnipotent God. Today I bless you with my thoughts, words, and behaviour. I bless you diligently, without laziness.

Prayer from Psalm 135

O Lord, I praise your name. Praising you is the key that unlocks divine healing. Please fill my mouth with praises, for this is the language of heaven. All pleasures are futile without God. I shall exalt you and bless you with word, action, and song. I will proclaim your greatness to everyone, and your fame shall spread over the earth and heaven.

You are the God who can do whatever he wills (v. 6)! You create wind and arrows of lightning, and you bring forth great clouds from the heavens (v. 7). You send wonders and signs, and for the sake of your people, you destroy great kings (vv. 9–10). You pour your compassion over your servants. You replace our mourning with joy and glory. You see and hear, and your heart beats with love for your people in pleasant and hard seasons. With celestial love, you have granted us the cross, the greatest redemption!

O God, I present to you my worship and hearty thanksgiving. You are worthy of all praise. Today, I shall urge myself and the rest of creation to praise the creator of earth, water, and air (vv. 19–20). Words of worship are like eternal jewels in a straw basket, a human body. Without worship, our lives are fading vapour. Today, let us praise and give thanks. Let us sing and praise the only one who is worthy of the greatest name. Today, I shall praise you and bless your name all day long. I shall give thanks to you in secret and in public.

~ Prayer from Psalm 136 ~

O Lord, you want me to contemplate your mercies and then praise you. You remind me of the richness of your grace. Then I praise you, for your mercy is forever!

You are all wise, omniscient, omnipotent, and the creator of all that exists. Your loving kindness is forever.

You are the greatest hero in kindness, a true legend in love, and the fountain of virtues. Your mercy is forever.

You are the compassionate mother, the physician of the spirit, and the lawyer of the oppressed. Your mercy is forever.

You are the engineer of creation, the everlasting artist, the provider of water to the seas, and the supplier of air to the atmosphere. Your mercy is forever.

You are the one who hugs the exhausted ones, who removes the burdens from the weary and heavy laden. Your mercy is forever.

You visited with a Samaritan woman. You delivered your people in the wilderness. You became the shelter for a woman caught in sin. Your mercy is forever.

You forgave Peter, transformed the life of Zacchaeus, and accept all who repent. Your mercy is forever.

You have forgiven me so many times and granted me so many second chances. Your mercy is forever.

On Friday you were hung on a cross; your blood was spilled for me. Your mercy is forever.

You take care of your church and your creation, both in pleasant and hard times. Your mercy is forever.

Today, I shall worship you and thank you for your holy covenant, as well as your grace. Your grace shall not be conquered, but shall continually reveal your mercy.

~ Prayer from Psalm 137 ~

The day of my painful failure is here. My enemy has left me weeping, in pain, and mourning (v. 1). Today is the day of my destruction and the devastation of my people; Jerusalem has fallen. Its fall is the end of my worship and perhaps my doctrine. It is the destruction of my strength and my dream that God rules over Jerusalem. I can no longer enter into the presence of the Lord to praise and sing (vv. 2–3). I can no longer speak of the greatness of God, for I am polluted with humiliation.

Jerusalem is the creed of my faith, the sign of God's faithfulness, and the dream of my dreams. Jerusalem is the kingdom of light, love, peace, and divine salvation. Jerusalem has been defiled. It has become dirty, crushed with death, and my speechless tongue now sticks to the roof of my mouth. Many hands are stretched out against the house of God, against Jerusalem and what it represents. We have hung Jerusalem on a cross. My pain is excruciating. With the destruction of Jerusalem, God has lost and my enemies have won!

But my heart is still in love. I still love my God and his Messiah. Even if they have crucified you, O Jerusalem, even if they have crucified my God, I shall not forget you (v. 5)! I shall not accept the sovereignty of Edom, Babylon, or their evil descendants. Instead, I will wait for the dawn of justice and the coming of the one who rewards. I shall treat Babylon as she treated me when she ended my joy (Rev 18:6) and destroyed my precious child. I shall call upon the Most High to remove all of her roots from my country.

I am not calling for a militant revenge, but for the elimination of destruction, terrorism, and every evil weapon raised against the creator. I do not want to see infants killed and brutal actions. Babylon is not a woman who brings forth children, but an image of evil whose children fight the Lamb, my redeemer.

When Christ rose from the dead, Babylon was sentenced to death. It was then that the Lord smashed this satanic civilization. I shall not fight with Babylon's weapons, but I shall believe in the death and eternal punishment of the enemies of the redeemer.

～ Prayer from Psalm 138 ～

O Lord, I know that you don't abandon the works of your hands. You take care of every soul and body. You are my protector whose mercy is forever (v. 8); your mercy is transgenerational; it is present today, tomorrow and throughout the generations. In all of my circumstances, you have been my shelter and my support.

Many arrogant people have surrounded me, and like roaring lions they have exalted themselves. I am as vulnerable as a lamb before their corrupt hearts and hungry teeth. I have fallen into an evil trap, but even here in fear, my heart has worshipped you. I have approached the consuming fire, and there my heart has been warmed and I have been filled with confidence. But their hearts are distant from you. They are like a freezing blizzard.

I have called out to God in the midst of my distress, and my heart has found its rest in you. You heard my cry and saw my torture. Then your mouth spoke and made promises (vv. 2, 4). You answered me and encouraged me (v. 3). You restored my life and saved me from the gloom of evil. You changed my circumstances.

Therefore my heart shall sing, praising your love. I shall fill my mouth with praises. The Most High has dealt with the wrath of my enemies. With his right hand, he delivered me (v. 7). With your faithful promises, you have overturned the balance. The left dish in the balance scale is fear, while the right side is praise. The contents of the dish of fear have evaporated, while the dish of praise is filled with songs of praise. I give thanks with all of my heart, every week and over all the span of my days (v. 1). All the kings of the earth, every village and every country worship you because of your words and deeds (v. 4).

~ Prayer from Psalm 139 ~

O Lord, you are a wonderful God! You are amazing in your knowledge, for even a hair does not fall from my head without your knowing it (vv. 1–6). Your knowledge covers everything and spreads everywhere like air. It is like water for a fish. You know everything about what I have done, what I am doing now, and what I am capable of doing. You know my weaknesses, my ignorance, every possibility, and all impossibilities. You know my demons and the evil person I could have become. You know every seed of goodness within me and the needed fertilizers for growing heavenly virtues. You know all the possibilities for every second of my life, every relationship, every breath, every thought, and everything that might happen to me.

You have known me since I was in my mother's womb, at her bosom, and in the hidden places. Before I was born, after I die, during my day, and during my night, you know me. You are present in every place (v. 7). Omniscient and omnipresent God, I surrender my life into your wise hands and place my small hand in your powerful one (v. 10).

I know that your understanding is far better and greater than mine; therefore I will seek your wisdom. I know that your knowledge is more comprehensive, more complete, and without error, and so I will obey your commandments. I know that you have knitted me with your knowledge, distinguished me with your understanding, covered me with your love, and kept me in your sight at all times. You are present with me every day, every moment, and in every situation. You shall always be my Creator and Father.

Examine me, O God, and test my heart. Examine my thoughts and check if any vain thoughts or paths dwell within me. Guide me on your eternal path (vv. 23–24).

~ Prayer from Psalm 140 ~

O Lord, deliver me from evildoers and protect me from oppressors (v. 1). Their hearts are like volcanoes of evil. Their tongues fight me like poisonous snakes (vv. 2–3). The arrogant hide their traps, ropes, nets, and ploys, waiting to devour me (v. 5). Death, murder, and destruction are one step away. Protect me, O Lord of the universe! Guard me from evil hands and save me from demonic conspiracies. Don't let their plots succeed. Don't grant them their evil wishes (v. 8) and don't let grief cover us.

I know that even truth that has been defeated for a moment is stronger than victorious evil that lasts for a century. But my moment has been too long; evil has covered my window. Every glance inflicts pain. If I no longer pray or act, then my country will become my grave.

But O Lord, you are my God. Therefore I lift up my prayers and requests in the power of your resurrection (v. 6). Even though I am only a sheep in the midst of a pack of wolves, I know that you are my strength and salvation. Even if I am a flower in the midst of foul garbage, I shall not give up my God-given aroma. By your grace, I shall forgive evildoers, but I will not tolerate evil, because you are my righteousness.

Let all evil, of every shape and kind fall. Let evil houses and those who uphold them fall. I will declare my war. My war is against evil and oppression, because I know that the Lord will vindicate the wretched poor. This is my path. O Lord, deliver me from evildoers and let me sit in your presence (v. 13).

～ Prayer from Psalm 141 ～

I lift up my hands like an evening sacrifice. My prayer is like incense inhaled by the eternal God (v. 2). The Lord has guarded my lips and mouth with celestial protection (v. 3).

I pray to the Lord. My prayer is like an oasis in the desert or a cup of cold water on a hellishly hot day. I seek forgiveness and wholeheartedly cry out, hoping to survive without any harm (v. 10). I zip my mouth and keep my heart busy with divine matters.

O Lord, I cry out to you! Please hurry! Listen to my voice and shout in my ears. I can neither hear nor see nor feel. I am afraid to move, even though I am just one bite away from Satan's mouth (v. 7)! Traps, snares, and nets surround me, and I am cornered. They have planned conspiracies and plots; many horrendous things could happen to me (vv. 9–10). A train of evil is rushing towards me while I am chained to the railroad tracks! Without you, Lord, I am falling from the clouds into a lake of fire. They have soaked me with petrol, and without you, they will strike a match! I scream to you with all my strength because death envelops me! Please hear my voice today, and deliver me from the trap they have set for me.

I lift up my hands like an evening sacrifice. May my prayer be acceptable incense before the Lord of eternity!

~ Prayer from Psalm 142 ~

O Lord, I thank you for the communal prayer in which we cry out, "Our Father in heaven." But I also need to cry out alone, and pour out my pain, alone before you (vv. 1–2). Had I poured out my complaints before my colleagues, they would have condemned me. Had evildoers heard them, they would have gloated over my humiliation. But I come alone before you to pray wholeheartedly and with all of my voice.

My soul has become sick from worry. I am suffering the pains of the land of death (v. 3). My friends and supporters have left me. In my need, I have been wounded and betrayed (v. 4). I don't cry out to make you hear me, or to justify my pain so that you might know about me, but so that through my tears I may discover the omniscient God. Then my eyes will be soothed by the fountain of blessing.

I don't shout aloud to declare my strength – to remind you of my victory over Goliath, to list my heroic acts, or even to declare my wisdom – but in my shouting, I hear the voice of the Lord of comfort. I don't shout because you are deaf. I don't ask you to look because you are blind. I don't seek mercy because you are harsh. But in my shouting, I discover self-denial. I discover that you are my shelter, my portion, and the one who liberates me from the chains of the spirit as well as from my many complaints.

I discover my portion in the land of the living (v. 5) when I discover the living God who rose from the dead. I trust that you shall show me mercy today (v. 7). You shall encourage me and do wonders.

～ Prayer from Psalm 143 ～

O Lord, hear my prayer and listen to my supplications (v. 1). I am a sinner, and my portion is death (vv. 1–2). I am crushed, and I sleep and rise in darkness (v. 3). I am exhausted from the labour of my spirit and the approach of death (v. 4). My country is full of persecution and merciless enemies. But I extend my arms to you, for you alone are my deliverer (v. 6). Don't hide your face from me, for without your sun, my hope fades (v. 7).

Hurry up and answer me! Hear me, so that my joy and peace may be restored. Teach me to do what pleases you, whether on the mountain or in the valley (v. 10). Whether I am in the desert (v. 6) or in a deep pit (v. 7), you lead me to the plains, for your mercy is calling out to me (v. 10). Teach me to do what pleases you in the different seasons of my life. Teach me to please you in my actions. Teach me to please you with the sweat of my brow and to challenge evil with my faith.

Pleasing you is eternal truth, but what others think of me is merely human opinion. If I please you, I don't care if my enemies or my friends are angry. But if you are angry, even though my supporters and friends are satisfied with me, then I am the biggest loser, even if I win all the world's treasures.

Teach me to be your disciple who sits in your heavenly council, listens to your voice, obeys your words, and spreads your kingdom day and night. Loving the Lord Jesus and glorifying the redeemer are the keys to pleasing you. Today, teach me to do what pleases you, for you alone are my deliverer.

⬤ Prayer from Psalm 144 ⬤

Blessed are the people that have a God like you (v. 15). In the morning I awaken and find that you have kept me all night, protected in your bosom. You give me food, and your generous cup of grace satisfies me. Your love has been unchanging all of my years, from infancy to old age.

Deliverance and mercy dwell with you. How beautiful is your salvation! Your arrows protect me from my enemies (v. 6). You deliver me from dangers by extending your arm to help me (v. 7). You open up to me the celebrations of heaven as I sing unto you (v. 9). You take care of the hair on my head, my barns, and my sheep. You are such a gracious God!

Don't grant me mere strength, but be my strength. Over the hardships of life, your strength always wins. Your people are like sturdy green plants (v. 12); you are our water, food, and shelter. We rejoice in your presence. By grace alone you bless our sons and daughters. When your kingdom dominates, our streets become empty of complaining, attacks, and outbreaks.

You have not only given us temporal blessings, but you have also sacrificed by dying to save us. You have shown us mercy and granted us your spirit. Today, you are with us. Tomorrow by your grace, we will be in your bosom. Be our king, be our judge, and be our shepherd. Blessed are the people who have a God like you.

~ Prayer from Psalm 145 ~

O God, how great thou art! Your people proclaim your greatness throughout generations (vv. 3–4). They continuously worship and contemplate your magnificent glory (v. 5). They tell of your abundant goodness and praise your justice (v. 7). They declare your merciful deeds and your longsuffering (vv. 8–9). They pronounce your glorious kingship and might (v. 11). Your dominion is forever. Your authority is greater than that of all powerful people (v. 13).

You help the fallen to rise and those who are bent to become upright (v. 14). The eyes of all look to you, hoping and seeking your help, because you are always compassionate (v. 15). You open your hand and satisfy many nations. The peoples of the earth are hungry for your love and generosity (v. 16).

You hear our prayer and supplication. You are near to all those who approach you in truth (v. 18). You bless those who fear you and hear their supplications; they shall be saved (v. 19). The mind of the church and its thoughts are greater than my individual mind. It is by your wisdom that your people are always protected. The brilliant minds of all generations show utter ignorance if they don't cling to Christ and join his people. The people of the Lord will always praise your holy name, hear your whispers, and see your hidden deeds with their eyes of faith; they will always value your salvation on the cross. Today, I shall join the choir of your beloved ones who worship you in truth and Spirit. Let my mouth be filled with praises! Let all human beings bless the God whose love and justice shall never dim or fail.

~ Prayer from Psalm 146 ~

Before I call others to praise you, my spirit will kneel down to honour you (v. 1). Make me today a choir with many songs and heavenly strings that praise you.

Before I explain the futility of human salvation, I bow down to worship you. Before I knock at the doors of the strong, I bend down to seek you. Before I start unpacking my worries, I sing and thank you.

You are the one who brings forth justice to the oppressed, feeds the poor, and releases the prisoners (v. 7). You freed the oppressed Joseph and Jeremiah from jail. In the lion's pit, you were with Daniel, and you released Peter from chains. Rhoda shared the good news that the Lord answers the prayers of the godly ones (Acts 12:6–19). You freed your people from the chains of oppressors, just as the prophets foretold.

You opened the eyes of the blind, and my own eyes have seen the glory of heaven. How many eyes have been bound by moral darkness? But with your light, they can see heavenly glories. You have straightened the bent ones and have relieved our worries (v. 8). You have searched for the marginalized and taken care of the widows, the orphans, and the strangers (v. 9). O Lord, rule over my country, and let the evil of the enemy end!

Prayer from Psalm 147

Singing unto the Lord of lords is pleasant.

He heals the broken-hearted (v. 3). He counts all the stars; none is without a name; none can escape from his care (v. 4). He covers the heavens with clouds, gives rain, and covers the mountainside with grass (v. 8). He gives the beasts their food and cares even for the youngest raven (v. 9).

He is not pleased with all the gold of the mountains, but only with those who plead for his mercy and love godliness (v. 10). Praise our God, for he has strengthened our gates (v. 13). He has granted us peace and grain and has filled our homes with food and drink (v. 14). He has also filled our hearts with peace and mercy, and with words that are sweeter than honey and more delicious than baklava.

He rules over creation and brings the frost. Then with the sun of his grace, we see the snow melt. He is wiser than wisdom, kinder than kindness, more beautiful than beauty. Whoever is in doubt can find guidance in him. He blesses generously and receives all who return and repent.

Singing unto our Lord is wise in youth and in old age. He distinguished us from all nations; therefore, we should never stop praising him, even in the midst of hardship. Today, it is right to praise the Lord! Let us honour the Lord of lords.

~ Prayer from Psalm 148 ~

Today is the day of the global choir; therefore let all creation worship and honour the Lord! O fiery angels, praise him. You witnessed the annunciation to Mary, the birth of Jesus, and the resurrection of Christ; therefore worship and praise him!

O sun and moon, remember that God fixed you in your position for the sake of his people and his leader, Joshua; therefore worship and praise him! O sun, you were clothed with darkness when God glorified his name during the days of Moses. During the days of Isaiah, you became a sign to Hezekiah. When Christ was crucified, you hid your light; therefore gather the stars and the planets today to praise and worship him!

O creatures of the world, come together to praise him. He made you an illustration of his wisdom and skill; therefore praise and worship him. Some animals he made as sacrifices that demonstrated his grace; therefore worship and praise him. O trees, he gave to you water, soil, and sun; you became a manger, a boat, and a cross for our Lord; therefore call all the plants to thank him, to praise and worship him! He gave unto you an eternal name, associating redemption with a wooden cross. Therefore worship and praise him! Christ ate fish and wheat; you became food to your creator; therefore magnify him!

But you, O human being, God has loved you more than all of his creation. No tongue can describe this love; therefore praise him. God became human, and we have become his people, not only by creation, but also through redemption. Hallelujah! Praise and worship him!

~ Prayer from Psalm 149 ~

When will the final war that ends all wars come? When will we destroy murder and wars before they destroy us? When will justice prevail in the East, West, North, and South? When will poverty be eradicated, along with greed? When will the orphan, the wretched, and those suffering deep pain be comforted? When will we sing a new song in which the crucified God is proclaimed? When will the constant noise of evil drums stop, among all the nations?

Your kind of peace, O Lord, is more costly than all wars. In wars, we lose soldiers and money. But stopping all wars will not happen without crucifying God!

I lift up the banner of my God, the Lord of lords, the one who is full of justice and love. I sing today while I am thinking of a new song and of the peace we long for (v. 1). I will dance and sing, knowing that God will fulfil his divine decree (v. 9). I will rejoice in the creator, and delight in the King of kings, the God of Jacob. I am gleeful, knowing that the kingdom of God will replace the problems of this world.

The God-King has come! He established his throne in a manger; then his throne became a cross. There he destroyed wars and ended death. There the fountain of life gushed out, full of praise and life to those who see and repent. Before the end of wars, sin must die; it will not die without the painful sacrifice of the crucified King.

Today I shall dream, sing, delight, and rejoice in the Lord! The earthly reality may look different, but in Christ, I can see and taste the end of oppression.

～ Prayer from Psalm 150 ～

Praise him everywhere, whether at home, at work, at church, or in a shop. Praise him in front of your computer and your television, and when you open Facebook. Praise him with ringtones of praise on your smart phone. Praise him while in your car, on a plane or on a train. Praise him when you sit or walk.

Praise him, using words that depict his divine beauty! Praise him in the morning, at noon, and in the evening. Praise him during seasons of joy or sadness, when you are angry and when you rest. Praise him during times of peace or war, security or turmoil. Praise him during seasons of loss or victory, and during weddings or imprisonment. Praise him with the angels, the poor, the rich, infants, men, women, and all human beings. Praise him with all instruments: tambourines, strings, flutes, bells, accordions, guitars and organs. Praise him with all your heart and your hands. Clap, sing, and dance! Praise him with words, with chords, and with every breath! Let praises explode like a volcano! O God, today I choose to praise you wholeheartedly, for my heart overflows with praise and my mouth is full of song.

Hallelujah!

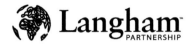 **Langham** PARTNERSHIP

Langham Literature and its imprints are a ministry of Langham Partnership.

Langham Partnership is a global fellowship working in pursuit of the vision God entrusted to its founder John Stott –

> *to facilitate the growth of the church in maturity and Christ-likeness through raising the standards of biblical preaching and teaching.*

Our vision is to see churches in the majority world equipped for mission and growing to maturity in Christ through the ministry of pastors and leaders who believe, teach and live by the Word of God.

Our mission is to strengthen the ministry of the Word of God through:
- nurturing national movements for biblical preaching
- fostering the creation and distribution of evangelical literature
- enhancing evangelical theological education

especially in countries where churches are under-resourced.

Our ministry

Langham Preaching partners with national leaders to nurture indigenous biblical preaching movements for pastors and lay preachers all around the world. With the support of a team of trainers from many countries, a multi-level programme of seminars provides practical training, and is followed by a programme for training local facilitators. Local preachers' groups and national and regional networks ensure continuity and ongoing development, seeking to build vigorous movements committed to Bible exposition.

Langham Literature provides majority world preachers, scholars and seminary libraries with evangelical books and electronic resources through publishing and distribution, grants and discounts. The programme also fosters the creation of indigenous evangelical books in many languages, through writer's grants, strengthening local evangelical publishing houses, and investment in major regional literature projects, such as one volume Bible commentaries like *The Africa Bible Commentary* and *The South Asia Bible Commentary*.

Langham Scholars provides financial support for evangelical doctoral students from the majority world so that, when they return home, they may train pastors and other Christian leaders with sound, biblical and theological teaching. This programme equips those who equip others. Langham Scholars also works in partnership with majority world seminaries in strengthening evangelical theological education. A growing number of Langham Scholars study in high quality doctoral programmes in the majority world itself. As well as teaching the next generation of pastors, graduated Langham Scholars exercise significant influence through their writing and leadership.

To learn more about Langham Partnership and the work we do visit **langham.org**